Praise for *How to Preach a Dangerous Sermon*

"Frank Thomas has written a passionate summons: amid the current destructive chaos of our society, there is an urgent need for moral imagination. Such imagination is the antithesis of 'diabolic' and 'idolatrous' imagination that is all to the fore in our public discourse and practice. Thomas fleshes out 'moral imagination' with close reflection on the practice of Robert F. Kennedy and Martin Luther King Jr. Before he finishes, Thomas shows how the urgency of 'moral imagination' belongs peculiarly to the work of the preacher. This book is a welcome call for gospel-grounded courage and truth about the neighbor issues in a way that refuses the self-serving fakery that dominates our public life."
—Walter Brueggemann, Professor Emeritus, Columbia Theological Seminary, Decatur, GA

"Timely and prophetic, *How to Preach a Dangerous Sermon* presents a homiletic essential for our churches today. Thomas insists that it is up to the preacher to recapture and reclaim the moral imagination of our nation so that the gospel's message of freedom is true for all people. With attention to specific figures whose witness models the qualities and characteristics of moral imagination, Thomas inspires the preacher toward powerful proclamation that both challenges and critiques any speech that subjugates or subordinates. *How to Preach a Dangerous Sermon* is a must read for preachers to recover and reimagine the leadership role of the church for the sake of justice for all."
—Karoline M. Lewis, Associate Professor of Biblical Preaching and the Marbury E. Anderson Chair of Biblical Preaching, Luther Seminary, St. Paul, MN; author, *She: Five Keys to Unlock the Power of Women in Ministry* (Abingdon Press)

"Open this book at your own risk. It is dangerous because in it, Frank Thomas tells the truth about the world and the moral imagination needed today in order for preaching to be redemptive. It is honestly prophetic and daringly hopeful, challenging us to move beyond a diabolical imagination to a moral one. It's not only Kennedy or King or Hall who can be dangerous communicators; Thomas reminds all of us that *we* are called to be dangerous too."
—Luke A. Powery, Dean of the Chapel, Duke University, Durham, NC

"Frank Thomas knows how to live dangerously in the pulpit—walking on the wild side with Jesus but in a beguiling, inviting way. Now Thomas encourages the rest of us preachers to preach with risk and delight, restoring the grand adventure of our vocation. This book is filled with wisdom and truth that Thomas has gained from his lifetime as one of our very best preachers. *How to Preach a Dangerous Sermon* is sure to be a regular in my preaching classes as I entice a new generation of preachers to be dangerous with Jesus."
—Will Willimon, author of *Conversations with Barth on Preaching* (Abingdon Press); Professor of the Practice of Christian Ministry, Duke Divinity School, Durham, NC; United Methodist Bishop, retired

"Warning: Preachers, if you are comfortable with the status quo of white privilege, patriarchy, hetero-normativity, and classism, do not read this book. If you are comfortable with sermon series that reduce the gospel to self-help acronyms, don't read this book. But if you have the courage to look honestly at our landscape and bring the moral imagination of the Christian tradition to bear on it, open these pages. Your sermons may never be the same again. But then again neither will the church—or the world—be the same anymore if enough of us follow Thomas's advice."
—O. Wesley Allen, Jr., Lois Craddock Perkins Professor of Homiletics, Perkins School of Theology, Southern Methodist University, Dallas, TX

"Frank Thomas's *How to Preach a Dangerous Sermon* is wisdom for preachers in an age of diabolical imagination and moral leadership bankruptcy. The foundational principles of Thomas's paradigm for moral imagination—equality, empathy, wisdom, and poetry—can inspire a revival of habits that have gone silent in our times: speaking truth and practicing good ethics. Thomas offers readers a timely project for nurturing hope within a politically chaotic commonwealth."
—Kenyatta R. Gilbert, Associate Professor of Homiletics, Howard University School of Divinity, Washington, DC; founding director, The Preaching Project; author, *Exodus Preaching: Crafting Sermons about Justice and Hope* (Abingdon Press)

"In this lucid and compelling book, Frank Thomas plumbs the depths of American moral rhetoric for insights that will help preachers. *How to Preach a Dangerous Sermon* provides new and dramatic ways in which the moral imagination in a democratic society can be nurtured by visionary, empathic, wise, and artistic preachers."
—John S. McClure, Charles G. Finney Professor of Preaching and Worship, Vanderbilt Divinity School, Nashville, TN

"*How to Preach a Dangerous Sermon* gifts the reader with a shared meeting point of Thomas's well-recognized pastoral sensibilities and critical analysis all in one text. This practical approach to preaching uses moral imagination to envision possibilities for our world and pulpits today. This is a timely text in uncertain times."
—Lisa L. Thompson, Assistant Professor of Homiletics, Union Theological Seminary, New York, NY

"Frank Thomas's *How to Preach a Dangerous Sermon* is now and will remain on my short list of books on preaching. It has the heft to deliver much of contemporary preaching in America from its milquetoast cultural captivity. The time is ripe for preachers to preach as if the soul of the church, preaching, the nations, and preachers depends upon it. I am persuaded that it does."
—Gregory Vaughn Palmer, Resident Bishop, Ohio West Episcopal Area, The United Methodist Church

FRANK A. THOMAS

Foreword by William J. Barber II

HOW TO

PREACH A

DANGEROUS

SERMON

Abingdon Press™

Nashville

HOW TO PREACH A DANGEROUS SERMON
Copyright© 2018 by Abingdon Press

This book is printed on acid-free paper.

Library of Congress Cataloging-in-Publication Data has been requested.

ISBN: 978-1-5018-5683-9

Scripture quotations unless noted otherwise are from the Common English Bible. Copyright © 2011 by the Common English Bible. All rights reserved. Used by permission. www.CommonEnglishBible.com.

Scripture quotations marked NRSV are taken from the New Revised Standard Version of the Bible, copy-right 1989, Division of Christian Education of the National Council of the Churches of Christ in the United States of America. Used by permission. All rights reserved.

Quotations in chapter 2 from "I've Been to the Mountaintop" by Martin Luther King Jr. are reprinted by arrangement with The Heirs to the Estate of Martin Luther King Jr., c/o Writers House as agent for the proprietor New York, NY. © 1968 Dr. Martin Luther King Jr. © renewed 1996 Coretta Scott King.

18 19 20 21 22 23 24 25 26 27—10 9 8 7 6 5 4 3 2 1
MANUFACTURED IN THE UNITED STATES OF AMERICA

To the memory of my brother, Frederick Erwin Thomas.
Home at last: where the wicked cease from troubling and the weary be at rest.

To the Memory of Sylvia Edith Shine Landau,
Who in a moment of profound suffering
Offered me this Jewish wisdom of the ages:

Blessed art thou,
O Lord Our God,
Who art sovereign,
Who gives life,
Who sustains us,
And brings us to this season

Moral imagination [is] the capacity to imagine something rooted in the challenges of the
real world yet capable of giving birth to that which does not yet exist.
John Paul Lederach

The whole creation waits breathless with anticipation for the revelation of God's sons and
daughters . . . the whole creation is groaning together and suffering labor pains up until
now . . .
Romans 8:19, 22 (CEB)

Also by the Author

America 2.0: A Christian Way Out of the Great Recession

The Choice: Living Your Passion Inside Out

The Choice: Living Your Passion Inside Out Companion Workbook

Introduction to the Practice of African American Preaching

The Lord's Prayer in Times Like These

Preaching as Celebration Digital Lecture Series and Workbook

Preaching with Sacred Fire: An Anthology of African American Preaching from 1750–Present

Spiritual Maturity: Preserving Congregational Health and Balance

They Like to Never Quit Praisin' God: The Role of Celebration in Preaching

What's Love Got to Do with It?: Love, Power, Sex, and God

What's Love Go to Do with It?: Love, Power, Sex, and God Companion Workbook

CONTENTS

Contents

Contents

THE TERRIBLE JOY OF DANGEROUS PREACHING

William J. Barber II

William J. Barber II is Founding President and Senior Lecturer of Repairers of the Breach and Architect of Forward Together Moral Monday Movement

I once heard someone say that preaching is a terrible joy, and I find that description true of my own experience. Whether I have preached to fifty or to fifty million, it has been nothing but joy to sense a call from the Spirit of God in my soul and train and prepare my mind to be used by God to declare eternal truths within temporal space. It is a humbling joy to have the assignment of communicating a *kairos* encounter in the midst of this world's *kronos*. When I consider my own finitude and flaws, it is a joy to even be considered a vessel of God. No wonder the Apostle Paul says in 2 Corinthians 4:6-7 (NRSV):

> For it is the God who said, 'Let light shine out of darkness,' who has shone in our hearts to give the light of the knowledge of the glory of God in the face of Jesus Christ. But we have this treasure in clay jars, so that it may be made clear that this extraordinary power belongs to God and does not come from us.

But this joy is tempered by one clear fact: preaching is also terrible and dangerous. It is terrible because, if we do our job well, preaching troubles and shakes the foundations of this world. True preaching dares to speak truth to powerful forces that have their own "alternative facts" and do not want to be challenged. This is why Paul went on to say in 2 Corinthians 4:8-12 (NRSV):

> We are afflicted in every way, but not crushed; perplexed, but not driven to despair; persecuted, but not forsaken; struck down, but not destroyed; always carrying in the body the death of Jesus, so that the life of Jesus may also be made visible in our bodies. For while we live, we are always being given up to death for Jesus' sake, so that the life of Jesus may be made visible in our mortal flesh. So death is at work in us, but life in you.

Paul knew as we also must know that to preach the gospel is, as a preacher friend frequently says, "to have a quarrel with the world. It is to be connected to the prophetic tradition that must always stand up to wickedness and injustice."

When the prophets of old said they were speaking the word of the Lord, they knew that amplifying God's truth would activate their adversaries. When Moses preached liberation and challenged Pharaoh to free the very slaves that had built Pharaoh's kingdom, Pharaoh did not bow. He resisted. Pharaoh went after Moses, the liberator, who dared speak the word of the Lord, insisting that Pharaoh's slavery and oppression were wrong. In fact, Moses's preaching was so dangerous that Pharaoh hunted him down. God called the prophet Isaiah to preach, but then told him that only 10 percent of the people would listen. Ezekiel had to tell leaders of the nation—both politicians and priests—that they were more like wolves than human beings when they pillaged the poor, the stranger, and the vulnerable. Jeremiah initially thought that if he preached, people would like him. But when he dared to speak truth to the King, he was castigated. Jeremiah wanted to quit. He complained that God had lied to him after he was thrown in a dungeon for daring to preach to the oppressive structure of his day. But God did not lie. The prophet simply failed to note that preaching is dangerous business.

Paul and Peter were jailed for preaching truth to power. Every apostle suffered for proclaiming the good news of Jesus. They challenged Caesar, a narcissistic tower-builder, who loved to place his picture on money and buildings to show his dominance. They knew that Caesar cared about the greedy and dismissed and despised the poor. But they also knew that their Lord had stood in his first sermon to say in Luke 4:18-19 (NRSV):

> The Spirit of the Lord is upon me,
> because he has anointed me
>   to bring good news to the poor.
> He has sent me to proclaim release to the captives
>   and recovery of sight to the blind,
>   to let the oppressed go free,
>   to proclaim the year of the Lord's favor.

In Luke's account of Jesus's inaugural sermon of Luke 4:28-30 (NRSV), we read:

> When they heard this, all in the synagogue were filled with rage. They got up, drove him out of the town, and led him to the brow of the hill on which their town was built, so that they might hurl him off the cliff. But he passed through the midst of them and went on his way.

But eventually they did kill Jesus because he preached the kingdom of love, care for the sick, the stranger, and the imprisoned over against the world's principles of greed, hate, division, and injustice. Jesus was killed because his preaching set him against the empire of his day.

Jesus never lied to those who would follow him about the consequences of committing to the ministry of the *kerygma*. He said, "If any want to become my followers, let them deny themselves and take up their cross daily and follow me" (Luke 9:23 NRSV). It should come as no surprise that when the power structure saw preachers who preached the real gospel come to town, they said, "These people who have been turning the world upside down have come here also" (Acts 17:6 NRSV).

The danger of preaching is found not only in the scriptural record, but also in the more recent history of our world. Frederick Douglass was hated by those who used religion to justify slavery because he preached a gospel that challenged injustice. At the end of his autobiography, Douglass notes:

What I have said respecting and against religion, I mean strictly to apply to the slaveholding religion of this land, and with no possible reference to Christianity proper; for, between the Christianity of this land, and the Christianity of Christ, I recognize the widest possible difference—so wide, that to receive the one as good, pure, and holy, is of necessity to reject the other as bad, corrupt, and wicked. To be the friend of the one, is of necessity to be the enemy of the other. I love the pure, peaceable, and impartial Christianity of Christ: I therefore hate the corrupt, slaveholding, women-whipping, cradle-plundering, partial and hypocritical Christianity of this land.[1]

William Lloyd Garrison, the evangelical abolitionist, was thrown in jail because he dared to preach the damnable truth that all people are created equal. When some advised him to stop he said, "I will be as harsh as truth, and uncompromising as justice... I am in earnest, I will not equivocate, I will not excuse, I will not retreat a single inch, and I will be heard."[2]

Martin Luther King Jr. preached in this same prophetic tradition. "He was God's trombone," writes homiletics professor Richard Lischer, "a true prophet who harnessed on behalf of social justice the black church's joy in the performed word."[3] For thirteen years on the public stage, King combined political acumen and biblical rhetoric in an American social struggle so riven with racial hatred that it is difficult to imagine today. At the heart of King's preaching was "the weapon of love," but this love was a strong love that demanded justice. Lischer says, "King didn't get in trouble for preaching love, but for preaching love in all the wrong places—places of power where ruthlessness and greed refused the challenge of truth."[4] For instance, just before King was killed, he preached a penetrating message after recounting the biblical parable of Lazarus and Dives to strikers in Memphis, just a few weeks before his assassination. King challenged America by saying that America was going to hell if it did not use its

---

1.   Frederick Douglass, *The Narrative of the Life of Frederick Douglass* (Mineola, NY: Dover, 1995), 71.

2.   William Lloyd Garrison, "I Will Be Heard, 1822–1835" in *The Letters of William Lloyd Garrison*, vol. I, ed. Walter M. Merill (Cambridge: Harvard Univeristy Press [Belknap], 1971).

3.   Richard Lischer, *The Preacher King: Martin Luther King, Jr. and the Word that Moved America* (New York: Oxford University Press, 1995), 12. Quote slightly altered.

4.   Quoted from sermon preached by Richard Lischer, "The Weapon of Love," at the Greenleaf Christian Church (Disciples of Christ) in Goldsboro, NC. Lischer locates the sermon in the late 1990s.

vast wealth to end poverty. Even though America built tall skyscrapers, he quoted the judgment of God on the nations in Matthew 25:42, "I was hungry and you fed me not. I was naked and you clothed me not."

Dangerous preaching is not simply a "critique from below," exposing the limits and weaknesses of the ruling class. In every generation, prophets of God warn the oppressor *and* the oppressed, exposing systemic evil and the ways it traps each of us in its sinister patterns. Dangerous preaching risks challenging those in power, but it also risks challenging the revolutionaries who would turn righteous indignation into hate, perpetuating the endless spiral of violence. The prophet Moses, who had grown up in Pharaoh's household, was angry at injustice, and the first time he saw a slave driver kill one of his fellow Hebrews, in his zeal, he killed the Egyptian. Forty years later, when God calls Moses to preach, the voice of God from the burning bush first affirms Moses's passion: "I have observed the misery of my people who are in Egypt; I have heard their cry on account of their taskmasters. Indeed, I know their sufferings" (Exodus 3:7-8 NRSV). God confronts the oppressed: the Hebrew children will not be liberated by the strength of Moses's hand, but by the word of the Lord.

"Let justice roll down," in Amos 5:24 (NRSV) is not a suggestion among suggestions, but a word from the Lord, the maker of heaven and earth. The prophet is not crafting a message to capture the imagination of the masses, but calling all people to be transformed by the renewal of their minds. Prophetic imagination introduces something beyond the available options—not left or right, liberal or conservative, but a new thing. A way out of no way. When Moses comes to the Red Sea with Pharaoh's army at his back and faces certain defeat, the word of the Lord compels Moses to step into the water—all the way up to his nose, the Rabbis say. Then God opens a path of dry land through the sea.

The word of the Lord is something more than carefully crafted words of human beings (though God does call us to work on the craft of preaching). Moses objects that he is not good with words. God counters: Moses already has the help he needs in his brother Aaron. Preaching isn't about us, but about God using us for something beyond us.

I was called to preach in my early twenties and worked hard on the craft at my first church in Martinsville, Virginia. But by the time I was thirty, I was crippled by an arthritic condition and had spent three months in a hospital bed. My doctors told me I'd never walk again. But from that hospital bed, I heard the call to preach again. Focused on my own limitations, I told God I couldn't do it. But God sent a church that came around me. Deacons who drove me wherever I needed to go, and assistants to do for me what I couldn't do for myself.

The prophetic imagination is a gift that comes to us from beyond ourselves, a message meant to shape, not reflect public opinion. When Jesus preaches "Woes" to the Pharisees in Matthew 23:3 (NRSV), he does not filter his statements through a popularity poll. The word of the Lord risks reminding the religious of the danger of focusing on minor religiosity— "tithing their mint and cumin while they neglect the weightier matters of the law."

Dangerous preaching challenges our established notions about religion and its place in society. Forces of injustice want the oppressed to believe there is no hope and they want their partners in oppression to never know repentance and change is possible. The sad truth is that religion often services this agenda, propping up the powerful, while persuading the oppressed that they are responsible for their lack. True preaching is dangerous because it dares to enter despair's territory and, as James A. Forbes once said, "Speaks to the death and death dealing systems of our time."[5] Dangerous preaching, in speaking to the death, offers hope. In Walter Brueggemann's words:

> Hope, on one hand, is an absurdity too embarrassing to speak about, for it flies in the face of all those claims we have been told are facts. Hope is the refusal to accept the reading of reality which is the majority opinion; and one does that only at great political and existential risk. On the other hand, hope is subversive, for it limits the grandiose pretension of the present, daring to announce that the present to which we have all made commitments is now called into question.[6]

---

5. Barber identifies these words in a private conversation between he and James A. Forbes.

6. Walter Brueggemann, *The Prophetic Imagination,* 2nd ed. (Minneapolis: Fortress Press, 2001), 65.

In this time in which we live, we see systemic racism, greed, poverty, classism, warmongering, and the war economy working in pernicious ways. In times like these, the recovery of dangerous preaching is a necessity. Cute, cuddly preaching that does not trouble or take the risk of the gospel is theological malpractice at best, heresy at worst. Recently Pope Francis said:

> When money, instead of man, is at the center of the system, when money becomes an idol, men and women are reduced to simple instruments of a social and economic system, which is characterized, better yet dominated, by profound inequalities. So we discard whatever is not useful to this logic; it is this attitude that discards children and older people, and is now affecting the young. We cannot wait any longer to deal with the structural causes of poverty, in order to heal our society from an illness that can only lead to new crises.[7]

The Pope was preaching dangerously. He was doing what Isaiah 11:4 (NRSV) says the prophet must do:

> with righteousness he shall judge the poor,
> and decide with equity for the meek of the earth;
> he shall strike the earth with the rod of his mouth,
> and with the breath of his lips he shall kill the wicked.

Only dangerous preaching can reshape the narrative of the empire and make real the possibility of transformation for our world.

How to Preach a Dangerous Sermon by Frank A. Thomas is desperately needed now and must become a major part of every preacher's library and a foremost text for all theological education. It is a careful and thoughtful exposition of the challenges of moral imagination in our time and how a preacher that seeks to be faithful must serve this present age in the context of danger and hope. Every social movement needs theological reflection and homiletical acumen. Thomas's book is dangerous and insightful theology combined with homiletical wisdom and training. It must be so because how can we preach dangerous sermons without dangerous theology and homiletical instruction?

---

7. Andrea Gagliarducci, "For Pope Francis, Loving Concern for the Poor Is Not Communism," *Catholic New Agency*, January 12, 2015, http://www.catholicnewsagency.com/news/for-pope-francis-loving-concern-for-the-poor-is-not-communism-54341/.

A CALL TO CONSCIENCE AND A DANGEROUS SERMON

It might be that I am a child of the sixties, and forever locked in a nostalgic timewarp. I carry the idealism, the hope, horror, grief, and the disappointment of the 1960s. At the beginning of the Montgomery Bus Boycott movement in 1955, Martin Luther King Jr. said that if black people marched nonviolently, and in Christian love, that when history books were written in future generations, historians would have to pause and say that a great race of black people lived who exhibited moral courage and stood up for their rights, thereby imbuing a new meaning into the world. Though I was eleven years old when King was killed, I believed it. When Robert F. Kennedy said that we could solve the poverty and racial problems of America, and we could do what the Greeks said long ago: "Tame the savageness of man and make gentle the life of this world,"[1] I believed it. When Jesus of Nazareth said in Matthew 5:9, "Blessed are the peace-makers, for they will be called children of God," I heard it in Sunday school and believed it and so much more of what Jesus said.

What has been difficult to reconcile, and yet also helps shape my moral imagination, is that when you say and do such things in a spirit of peace-making, nonviolent Christian love; attempt to solve the inequities of the poor; and bridge race relations, you are likely to be persecuted, if

---

1. Robert F. Kennedy, "Remarks on the Assassination of Martin Luther King Jr.," *American Rhetoric*, February 15, 2017, http://www.americanrhetoric.com/speeches/rfkonmlkdeath.html.

not outright killed. Why is it that Martin Luther King Jr. who adopted and practiced nonviolence, was persecuted and subsequently killed by violence? Why is it that when Robert F. Kennedy determined and worked to resolve poverty and race relations in an abundantly wealthy nation, he was killed? What does our nation lose from its moral imagination when such voices are silenced? We have not yet recovered from the loss of Kennedy and King, and many more like them, who lived dangerous lives for the values of peace, love, freedom, justice, and equality for all.

We find ourselves in a time when white nationalism, patriarchy, and white supremacy are installed—and massively empowered—at the highest levels of American government. In this environment, without the leading voices of Kennedy and King, it seems even more dangerous to preach the message of peace and freedom for all. It is dangerous in this white-supremacist America to move the sphere of one's moral concern out of the circumference of one's group, and include the outcast, stranger, marginalized, and hated. It may or may not get you killed, but it certainly will get you persecuted; fired; harassed; labeled "enemy," "traitor," and such, especially if you choose to preach dangerous sermons.

If persecution is often the consequence of moral imagination, the question must be asked: Why preach from the moral imagination? Why engage such risk? Martin Luther King Jr. suggested in his April 3, 1967, speech in New York City, "Beyond Vietnam," that it was tremendously difficult to move against conformist thought and the resultant apathy in the world and one's own soul. King, against civil rights legislator and hero President Lyndon Baines Johnson and the American government, announced his opposition to the Vietnam War. King said, quoting the Executive Committee of Clergy and Laity Concerned about Vietnam, "There comes a time when silence is betrayal."[2] Maybe we preach moral imagination because some form of a call to conscience stirs, or the sense that if one does not stand up for what is right, the nation loses its moral footings, or because of one's faith tradition, or in my case, because Jesus says, "love your neighbor as yourself." Maybe it is one of these or some combination of all of these.

---

2. Martin Luther King Jr., "4 April 1967 Beyond Vietnam, New York, N.Y." *King Encyclopedia*, accessed August 31, 2017, http://kingencyclopedia.stanford.edu/encyclopedia/documentsentry/doc_beyond_vietnam/.

What I know is that if I do not preach from moral imagination, something vital in the nation and in my person is lost. If at least some of my sermons are not dangerous, I lose a piece of my integrity.

In times of unabashed misogyny, xenophobia, "alternative facts," "fake news," open vitriol, racism, and hate, if I do not preach and act out the fundamental truth that God loves all, then I lose my self-respect. If I do not reach deep into moral imagination and envision a world beyond the supremacist, nationalistic, and oppressive culture in which I live, then I have sacrificed my principles and embarrassed my calling as a minister of the gospel. If I participate in preaching smooth patriotism and evangelism divorced from the lack of material prospects of the marginalized, or preach an over-promised gospel of wealth and prosperity that benefits the few instead of a dangerous gospel to serve the poor, then when I lay my head on the pillow at night, I am a non-Christian and nonperson. I must call myself to conscience.

From my faith tradition as an African American Christian; my participation in struggles for equality and justice in America; and my respect for the long lineage of many and varied people who have worked for freedom and justice, often persecuted and killed; I want to list the four qualities of the moral imagination that we so desperately need. I will more fully discuss these qualities in the upcoming pages:

1. Envision equality and represent that by one's physical presence

2. Empathy as a catalyst or bridge to create opportunities to overcome the past and make new decisions for peace and justice

3. Sources of wisdom and truth in ancient texts, the wisdom of the ages

4. The language of poetry and art that lifts and elevates the human spirit by touching the emotive chords of wonder, hope, and mystery

Many would call preaching from moral imagination prophetic preaching, or preaching from the prophetic imagination. Brueggemann correctly and pointedly declares that the prophet brings to light "public expressions of those very hopes and yearnings that have been denied so long and suppressed so deeply."[3] Brueggemann further explains prophetic imagination by alluding to a novel entitled *Imagining Argentina*. The key character, Carlos Rueda, has the miraculous gift of creating futures by acts of anticipatory imagination. Brueggemann quotes *Imagining Argentina*:

> Confronted with evidence of the miraculous, Carlos' friends nevertheless remain skeptical, convinced that Carlos cannot confront tanks with stories, helicopters with mere imagination. They can only see the conflict in terms of fantasy versus reality. Carlos, on the other hand, rightly grasps that the contest is not between imagination and the real, but between two types of imagination, that of the generals and that of their opponents. The nightmare world of torture and disappearance of bodies is inseparable from the generals' imagination of what Argentina and Argenitnes are.[4]

Carlos envisioned that his imagination was stronger than the imagination of the state. In writing this book, these words are exactly my sentiment: the moral imagination of a world of peace and justice is stronger than white supremacy's imagination of who and what we are.

Therefore, I do not have a problem with association and nomenclature of Brueggemann. I just wonder, considering the legitimacy and credence given to white nationalism and white supremacy in recent years, if additional creative frameworks and techniques of preaching are needed to face this hour. It might be that the traditional nomenclature of prophetic preaching and prophetic imagination is sufficient. For me, when I researched the term *moral imagination*, it spoke fresh to me and summoned me to write this book.[5] If the prophetic nomenclature works better for you, then by all means, please use it. I am not sure, but my sense is

---

3. Walter Brueggemann, *The Prophetic Imagination*, 2nd ed. (Minneapolis: Fortress Press, 2001), 65.

4. Ibid., xix.

5. For important theological sources of the term moral imagination, Dale Allison, *The Sermon on the Mount: Inspiring Moral Imagination* (New York: Herder and Herder, 1999); Susan E. Babbit, *Impossible Dreams: Rationality, Integrity, and Moral Imagination* (Boulder, CO: Westview, 1996); William P. Brown, *The Ethos of the Cosmos: The Genesis of Moral Imagination in the Bible* (Grand Rapids: Eerdmans, 1999); Carol A. Newsom, *The Book of Job: A Contest of Moral Imaginations* (New York: Oxford University Press, 2003); Edward Stevens, *Developing Moral Imagination: Case Studies in Practical Morality* (New York: Sheed and Ward, 2008).

that I am providing a concurrent framework and technique for preaching based in the challenge of preaching in this unique time.

This book then is a summons to readers, a clarion call to conscience and the dangerous preaching of moral imagination. Many are wondering what and how to preach given the massive rise of white supremacy and white nationalism. There are even preachers openly endorsing, supporting, and engaging these forces to forward their pet moral agenda, while ignoring the broader call of justice, compassion, and inclusion for the vulnerable and marginalized. The temptation is to get locked into a kind of despair that leads to inactivity, or anger and rage that lead to unprincipled and unproductive action. Many clergypersons choose to be silent, realizing that "politics" is polarizing, and the best thing is not to offend anyone by saying or doing anything that remotely could be conceived of as "controversial." Some preachers resort to name-calling and condescending rhetoric that titillates an assenting and fawning audience, but effects no real change because it does not call people to the depths of their moral imagination for the potential of sustained and effective action and resistance. As a thought-leader in preaching, neither of these alternatives is attractive to me, and therefore this book is meant to help preachers preach dangerous sermons based upon the clarity of their moral imagination for the good of the individual and community.

With the help of many sources and writers, I explain what is moral imagination, and why imagination rules the world. Then, I offer examples of moral imagination from the legacies of Robert F. Kennedy and Martin Luther King Jr., and develop four qualities of the moral imagination. Next, I illustrate how to preach dangerous sermons from the moral imagination by fleshing out the beginnings of a homiletic method based in the four qualities of the moral imagination, and offer a sermon as an example. The final word is given to the memory and legacy of activist, professor, and master-preacher Prathia L. Hall, who leaves a giant testimony of moral imagination. In summary, I want to offer my definition of preaching from moral imagination: *Moral imagination is the ability of the preacher, intuitive or otherwise, in the midst of the chaotic experiences of human life and existence, to grasp and share God's abiding wisdom and ethical truth in order to benefit the individual and common humanity.*

Finally, one does not develop moral imagination alone. One is helped by prophets, guides, chaperones, teachers, coaches, professors, leaders, advisers, parents, family, friends, spouses, children, church members, colleagues, students, prayer warriors, and so on. You will forgive me for saying a collective "Thank you." Many of you know who you are and because I have called your name in other books, I will not call you now, except to add a special "Thank you," to my editor, Connie Stella; to Abingdon Press for work and diligence to bring this manuscript to life; to Amelia Walker for the administrative support; to my friend for life, L. L. Welborn; and to my wife, Joyce Scott Thomas, for all of the encouragement and patience with my scholarship. I love you all.

I close with one of my favorite definitions of moral imagination by John Paul Lederach in his book *The Moral Imagination: The Art and Soul of Building Peace.* He defines moral imaginatioin as "the capacity to imagine something rooted in the challenges of the real world yet capable of giving birth to that which does not yet exist."[6]

In resistance and hope,
Frank A. Thomas
November, 2017
Indianapolis, Indiana

---

6.   John Paul Lederach, *The Moral Imagination: The Art and Soul of Building Peace* (New York: Oxford University Press, 2005), 29.

THE CRITICAL VALUE OF MORAL IMAGINATION

> *So the great contest... is not for human economic interests, or human political preferences, or even for human minds—not at the bottom. The true battle is being fought in the... human imagination. Imagination does rule the world.*
>
> *Russell Kirk*

In a poem entitled, "Democracy," protesting the lack of democracy for African American people, Langston Hughes, the prolific African American poet of the Harlem Renaissance wrote of freedom as a strong seed that was

> Planted
> In a great need.[1]

What Hughes meant, at least in part, is that freedom is deeply planted in the hearts and imaginations of those who have been denied freedom and equality. There is a basic and perverse strain of self-preservation in human nature that those who have freedom protect their privilege, not just against "tyranny," but also from others in a society deemed unworthy of the rituals and benefits of freedom. Human nature tends to conserve and constrict freedom and equality to the benefit of one's group, however that

---

1. Arnold Rampersad, ed. and David Roessel, assoc. ed., *The Collected Poems of Langston Hughes* (New York: Knopf, 1994), 289.

group is defined, whether composed around morals, politics, economics, race, nationality, gender, sexual orientation, region, or religion. It is human nature to limit freedom to one's group, and be perfectly contented that freedom is limited, restricted, and privileged to a few. As human beings, we often rationalize and blame the lack of freedom on fate, or some innocuous fault, deficiency, or flaw in the character, person, and humanity, individually or collectively, of the unfree. For the most part, the moral imagination of the free is limited, and the practical result based upon that limitation in a culture or nation is that only a few lives matter.

In a strange twist of fate, freedom is kept free by the moral imagination of those who do not have the rituals and benefits of freedom. Freedom is kept free by the moral imagination of those who, by sentiments and actions of protest, continue to push, prod, poke, and break the boundaries and preset limits of freedom. If we are looking for an example, I might suggest that America would still have segregation and signs of "white" and "colored" without the civil rights movement. America had to be carried, kicking and screaming every inch of the way, by the sacrifice, blood, and death of many innocent people to move America toward freedom and equality for all in the mid-twentieth century. Therefore, if we are looking for freedom, it is important to look to the moral imagination of the marginalized, disenfranchised, and vulnerable in any society and culture, along with those who have the moral imagination to understand, empathize, and work for the freedom of those outside of their group. My chief concern is that it takes moral imagination to envision freedom for more than ourselves or for our particular group. Because of a lack of such moral imagination, freedom and equality are often granted to a few and found sorely lacking in American culture and society, and around the globe for that matter.

Imagination Rules the World

It is important to note that the phrase "moral imagination" was coined by Edmund Burke in his *Reflections on the Revolution in France*. The simplest definition of moral imagination comes to us from conservative writer Russell Kirk: "The apprehending of right order in the soul and right order in the commonwealth."[2] According to Kirk, moral imagination is the ability to "perceive ethical truth, and abiding laws in the seeming chaos of many events."[3] Kirk argues that "imagination rules the world" because imagination molds the clay of our sentiments and understandings. While it is often assumed that human beings understand the world through calculations, formulas, and logical syllogisms, the reality is that we understand the world through images, myths, and stories, and thereby, comprehend our relationship to God, nature, others, and the self.[4] Kirk suggests that "not pure reason, but imagination—the high dream or the low dream—is the moving force in private and public life."[5] Kirk explains:

> All great systems, ethical or political, attain their ascendency over the minds of men (human beings) by virtue of the imagination; and when they cease to touch the chords of wonder and mystery and hope, their power is lost, and men (human beings) look elsewhere for some set of principles by which they may be guided.[6]

According to Burke, when moral imagination is lacking, human beings are cast forth "from this world of reason, and order, and peace and virtue, and fruitful penitence, into the antagonist world of madness, discord, vice, confusion, and unavailing sorrow."[7] Burke suggested that the

---

2. Russell Kirk, as the title of his memoirs suggests, *The Sword of Imagination*, fought a fifty-year spiritual, moral, and cultural war against liberalism and modernity in his writing, speaking, and editing. He waged war in the world of images and ideas where the most contested battleground was the imagination of the rising generation. See Russell Kirk, "The Moral Imagination," *The Russell Kirk Center for Cultural Renewal*, accessed August 31, 2017, http://www.kirkcenter.org/detail/the-moral-imagination/.

3. Darrin Moore, "Russell Kirk and the Swords of Imagination," *The Imaginative Conservative*, May 16, 2012, http://www.theimaginativeconservative.org/2012/05/russell-kirk-and-swords-of-imagination.html.

4. Gleaves Whitney, "The Swords of the Imagination: Russell Kirk's Battle with Modernity," *The Imaginative Conservative*, December 14, 2015, http://www.theimaginativeconservative.org/2015/12/timeless-essay-the-swords-of-the-imagination-russell-kirks-battle-with-modernity.html.

5. Jon M. Fennell, "What Is the Moral Imagination?" *The Imaginative Conservative*, April 11, 2016, http://www.theimaginativeconservative.org/2016/04/what-is-the-moral-imagination.html.

6. Moore, "Russell Kirk and the Swords of Imagination."

7. Kirk, "The Moral Imagination."

spirit of religion has long sustained moral imagination and also moral imagination must be expressed afresh from age to age.

Besides moral imagination, Kirk posits four more "swords of imagination": Historical imagination, political imagination, poetic imagination, and prophetic imagination.[8] Though it would be interesting to further delineate these forms of imagination, what is more relevant to our work herein is several forms of imagination that Kirk articulates in response to the challenge of modernity. In an article on Kirk entitled, "The Swords of the Imagination: Russell Kirk's Battle with Modernity," Gleaves Whitney interprets Kirk's understanding of the real conflict of the modern age:

> The old image of the human person as a wayfaring pilgrim, as a noble but tragic figure metaphysically secure in the great chain of being, was fast fading from modern consciousness.... What took its place? New dehumanizing images—of 'man the machine,' of 'man as the cunning animal,' of a creature who no longer enjoyed a privileged place in the cosmos and no longer had recourse to a personal, merciful God.[9]

According to Kirk, some modernists responded to this metaphysical disorientation by developing the "idyllic imagination." The term, "idyllic imagination," coined by Irvin Babbitt, rejects old dogmas and old manners and rejoices in the notion of emancipation from duty, honor, decorum, standards, and convention and "escapes into an endless stream of exciting sensation and sensuality."[10] It attempts to perfect human beings and human institutions without a transcendent deity and eternal destiny. Following Jean-Jacques Rousseau, the desire is to create utopia. Kirk mentions that many young people of the sixties and seventies in America became "infatuated" with the idyllic imagination, but were disappointed

---

8. Whitney, "The Swords of the Imagination: Russell Kirk's Battle with Modernity." Kirk said that those whose province is humane letters, and who would embark on a crusade to fight the "errors of their time" should be equipped not with just one but five "swords of the imagination." They need the *historical* imagination to understand where humankind has been. They need the *political* imagination to know what humankind can do. They need the *moral* imagination to discern what the human person ought to be. They need the *poetic* imagination to perceive how human beings should use their creative energies. And they need the *prophetic* imagination to divine what human beings will be, given the choices they make.

9. Ibid.

10. Moore, "Russell Kirk and the Swords of Imagination."

and disillusioned because utopia literally means "no place," for, in fact, "it has never been nor will it ever be."[11]

In response to modernity, another kind of imagination closely related to the idyllic imagination is the "idolatrous imagination," posited by Vigen Guroian.[12] Idolatrous imagination fixates on, and inappropriately honors, celebrity culture that is full of famous "heroes" from sports, music, movies, and television. Often, these celebrities are prepackaged and sold by mass marketing and mainstream corporate media. Rather than enjoying these entertainments in moderation, obsessions with idolatrous imagination crowds out worthy everyday heroes such as teachers, firefighters, first responders, and so on. According to Moore, what is also lost is "valuable leisure time in which an individual's genuine and optimal personality can be cultivated."[13]

Finally, once individuals become bored or disillusioned with the idyllic and idolatrous imagination, many turn to the diabolic imagination. The diabolic imagination strips human beings of the image of God. Human beings are an "accidental collection of atoms, a bundle of nerve endings striving for pleasure and shrinking from pain."[14] Quoting T.S. Eliot in lectures entitled, "After Strange Gods," Kirk defines the diabolic imagination as that which delights in the subhuman and the perverse. For Kirk, death, destruction, cynicism, and despair are the raw materials of the diabolic imagination and Marquis de Sade is its modern prototype.[15] The diabolic imagination dominates most popular fiction, television, and theaters, including pornography, because it panders to the lust for violence, destruction, cruelty, and sensational disorder. Much of this is standard fare on prime-time television, in Hollywood scripts, and the commercial airwaves

---

11. Whitney, "The Swords of the Imagination: Russell Kirk's Battle with Modernity."

12. Vigen Guroian, "Moral Imagination, Humane Letters, and the Renewal of Society," May 12, 1999, The Heritage Foundation, http://www.heritage.org/research/lecture/moral-imagination-humane-letters-renewal-of-society.

13. Moore, "Russell Kirk and the Swords of Imagination."

14. Whitney, "The Swords of the Imagination: Russell Kirk's Battle with Modernity."

15. Ibid.

that result in the fact that "the ceremony of innocence is drowned."[16] The diabolic imagination is singularly lacking in moral imagination.

In summary, Kirk ruminates on the decline and fall of the once-great Roman Empire. Kirk notices that Diocletian, who had become master of the Roman Empire, was compelled to starve himself to death in his own palace, and wonders if there is much hope for Western Civilization at the close of the second millennium. He posits that the "cake of custom was being trampled underfoot near the end of the twentieth century, as much as the cake of custom had been broken about the beginning of the fourth century."[17] Kirk admits that the understanding of vanquished civilizations might postpone destruction, but no human being could know the future, and events were finally in the hands of God. Whatever the outcome, Kirk believed the ultimate battle for survival would take place in the imagination:

> The real conflict of our age is between opposed types of imagination. . . . There are the idyllic imagination of Rousseau, the diabolic imagination of Sade, the leveling imagination of Marx, the moral imagination of Burke . . . and other species that might be distinguished. . . . So the great contest in these declining years is not for human economic interests, or for human political preferences, or even for human minds—not at the bottom. The true battle is being fought in the human imagination. Imagination does rule the world.[18]

For Kirk, the most contested battleground is for the imagination of the rising generation.

In my study of Burke, Kirk, Babbit, and so on, I was surprised how much agreement I had with the concept of moral, idyllic, idolatrous, and diabolical imagination. Generally, I find most conservative ideas not inclusive of my interests and my reality, principally because the most recent expressions of the conservative movement have articulated opposition to support for diversity, social programs, equal rights for women, environmentalism, public education, LGTBQ communities, ethnic minorities,

---

16. Kirk, "The Moral Imagination."

17. Whitney, "The Swords of the Imagination: Russell Kirk's Battle with Modernity."

18. Ibid.

a woman's right to choose, Planned Parenthood, gun control, and so on. The "traditional values" of the conservative movement never seem to include critical analysis of race, misogyny, patriarchy, immigration, discrimination, capitalism, and so on. Many conservatives lament and disdain the "identity politics" of contemporary social movements. This argument is offensive because white supremacy has played identity politics for generations upon generations. In regard to African Americans, slavery, Jim Crow, and even mass incarceration are based on white identity politics.

George Lakoff, in his book, *Moral Politics: How Liberals and Conservatives Think*, helped me understand my fundamental disagreement with conservative ideology. Lakoff articulates the "Moral Order Metaphor," which projects a dominance hierarchy onto the moral domain and creates a corresponding hierarchy of legitimate moral authority, assuming that the most moral should rule. This hierarchy is considered as just, that power *should* and *by right* rest with the "most moral." Lakoff establishes the following hierarchy that flows from the "Strict Father morality," of conservatives:

> God over Human Beings; Human beings over Nature; Adults over Children; The Rich over The Poor (and hence, Employers over Employees); Western Culture over Non-Western Culture; Our Country over Other Countries...Men over Women; Whites over Nonwhites; Straights over Gays; Christians over Non-Christians.... In each case, the hierarchy limits the freedom of those lower on the hierarchy by legitimating the power of those higher on the hierarchy...a large portion of conservative political policies flow from the conservative moral order.[19]

I disagree with the moral imagination of the conservative moral order and the hierarchy, dominance, and oppression that follow. As an African American person, why would I agree to this moral order that asserts my own moral subservience, or as Jay-Z says, "participate in my own

---

19. George Lakoff, *How Liberals and Conservatives Think*, 3rd ed. (Chicago: University of Chicago Press, 2016), 431. Lakoff argues that liberals and conservatives have very different moral systems, and that much of the political discourse of conservatives and liberals derives from their moral systems. Both subscribe to the metaphor of the Nation-as-Family. Contemporary conservatives follow a Strict Father morality and contemporary liberals follow a Nurturant Parent Morality.

invisibility?"[20] I cannot support any party, ideology, religion, moral order, and so on that delegitimizes my full humanity in the human order. It is the height of injustice and an insult to demand that the maligned support those that question and deny their full humanity.

White supremacy and white privilege are the default positions of America and remain fundamentally unaddressed, basically because many, especially whites, vehemently deny their very existence. Some deniers go so far as even to argue that black racism is a bigger problem than white racism. This denial generally makes most conservative writers, and the terrible public policy that is often the result for minorities, not representative of my viewpoints and interests. Despite all of this difference, there is important truth in the concepts of moral, idyllic, idolatrous, and diabolical imagination. One of the goals of this book is to apply idyllic, idolatrous, and diabolical imagination to American life, and discern and activate the moral imagination of America in the twenty-first century, starting with the moral imagination of preachers.

American Moral Imagination in the Twenty-First Century

The moral imagination of America is dominated primarily by the idolatrous and diabolical imagination. American moral imagination will always eventually slide to the idolatrous and diabolical imagination as long as ritual of benefit and freedom are the domain of a few. I want the reader to clearly understand the reasoning behind my judgment that America's moral imagination is dominated by the idolatrous and diabolical imagination by looking at four critical ideas: (1) a balanced view of the American character and identity, (2) the rituals and benefits of freedom for a few, (3) the quest to perfect our Union, and (4) white supremacy and the refusal of equality.

First, it is critically important in discerning the moral imagination of America that we take a balanced view of American cultural identity,

---

20. Jay-Z, *Decoded* (New York: Spiegel and Grau, 2011), 161.

and therefore the character of America. The fundamental cultural myth of America is a city set on a hill, blessed by God to be the light of the world, with the spiritual values of optimism, hard work, frugality, capitalistic economic striving, and a virgin land as assets to bring the kingdom of God to earth.[21] This cultural myth formed a "centrality" that bound the American nation together in common habits, language, beliefs, and values. Even as cultural myth binds a people together, it also limits their perspective, and in some sense blinds them. The blindness in regard to the cultural myth of America is found by asking who in the society is excluded, marginalized, subjugated, domesticated, and in some cases, even defined as less than human. How does the cultural myth of America function in regard to the respect and treatment of indigenous cultures and people, including groups denied freedom, equality, citizenship, economic participation, voting rights, and so on, in other words, the domination of subjected people?

Scavan Bercovitch, the Canadian literary and cultural critic, who was a leader and influential figure in the field of American Studies, presents a true and balanced view of American character and cultural identity. Bercovitch comments on the twin dynamics of empire, the creative energy and the violence of America:

> As I followed its (American cultural myth) changing terms of identity (Puritan errand, national mission, Manifest Destiny, the dream) the windings of language turned out to be matters of history. "America" as an act of symbolic appropriation came alive to me as the twin dynamics of empire: on one hand, a process of violence unparalleled (proportionately) by even the Spanish conquistadors and sustained in the twentieth century by a rhetoric of holy war against everything un-American; on the other hand, an unleashing of creative energies—enterprise, speculation, community building, personal initiative, industry, confidence, idealism, and hope—unsurpassed by any other modern nation. What I discovered in the interconnections between violence and culture formation was transcendence in action: 'America,' an interpretation, through which the worlds out there had been triumphantly repressed, rhetorically and historically—first, by the myths of their inhabitants ("savage," "primitive") attended by the facts

---

21. For a deeper treatment of "a city set on a hill," please see Frank A. Thomas, *American Dream 2.0: A Christian Way Out of the Great Recession*, "Section One: The Rise and Fall of the American Dream" (Nashville: Abingdon Press, 2012), 1–27.

of genocide and then by symbols of the land ("virgin," "wilderness") attended by the creation of the United States as "America."[22]

Just as it is difficult for an individual to have an honest and balanced view of themselves, given the complexity of motives, drives, rationalizations, self-interest, and morals in any action or decision, it is very difficult for most Americans to take a balanced view of America. Most tend to view America from the perspective of patriotism and laud the greatness of America, or, on the other hand, with a view to conquest and oppression, and therefore extol the violence and cruelty of America. When we look at the total picture of American character, America has both released more creative energy into the world than any modern nation in history, and yet, has also been imperialistic and violent on an unparalleled level. Often, America celebrates the industry, confidence, idealism, and hope of America, yet ignores the effects of imperialism, violence, discrimination, racism, slavery, misogyny, genocide, and the conquest of indigenous people. Americans have a very difficult time coming to terms with the twin dynamics of empire, often residing in the concept of American exceptionalism and leading to American imperialism. Without a balanced view of American greatness and American violence, we can never accurately ascertain the true moral imagination of America.

The second aspect of discerning the moral imagination of America is to accept and come to terms with the truth that the ritual and benefit of freedom of America has *always* been restricted to a few certain privileged groups within American culture. In examining the plight of mid-nineteenth-century feminists as one of those excluded from freedom, Bercovitch points out:

> When William Arthur spoke of "the American," he was not thinking of people like Margaret Fuller—or for that matter, of Fredrick Douglass, Black Hawk, Rabbi Isaac Meyer Wise, of John England, the Catholic Bishop of South Carolina...[23]

22. Sacvan Bercovitch, *The American Jeremiad* (Madison: University of Wisconsin Press, 1978), 978–79.

23. Sacvan Bercovitch, "Investigations of An Americanist," in *The Journal of American History,* vol. 78, no. 3 (Dec 1991), 160.

The truth is historically, and even at that this present moment, there have been and are people marginalized and excluded from being "Americans." While we must acknowledge that progress has been made, we must also acknowledge that freedom has been painfully slow. American rituals and benefits of freedom have been intended for a few because certain groups were and are considered less than "Americans" and "other." Hence the oppressive and dismissive language of "take our country back" and defining certain groups as "real Americans."

Michael Novak argues that the "adolescent American dream is ethnocentric," that is, "its primary symbols are white Anglo American, Protestant, and male." [24] In accordance with American exceptionalism, Novak concludes that "the central axis of world history, according to this [American] dream, pivots on the history of the Anglo-American race." [25] Notice Novak's use of the word "adolescent," meaning that the American Dream can mature to include, based upon protest and dissent across time, some of the very people who were once excluded, and often has, more prominently with European immigrants than with anyone else. This brings us to the third factor in discerning the moral imagination of America, perfecting the Union.

In my book *American Dream 2.0: A Christian Way Out of the Great Recession*, I detail the media-created firestorm of March 13, 2008, and beyond created by the airing of sound bites of the sermons of Jeremiah Wright Jr. [26] For many, Wright's comments had the potential to decimate the presidential hopes of then-candidate Barack Obama. Obama was forced to deliver a speech entitled "A More Perfect Union" on March 18 in Philadelphia, Pennsylvania. Reminiscent of John F. Kennedy's 1960 presidential campaign speech before Protestant leaders to address the issue of his Roman Catholic faith and the separation of church and state, Obama's address was highly anticipated and certain to be highly scrutinized. The issue for Obama was squarely race, with all of the tension and anxiety that race in America engenders.

---

24. Michael Novak, *Choosing Our King: Powerful Symbols in Presidential Politics* (New York: McMillan, 1974), 290.

25. Ibid.

26. Thomas, *American Dream 2.0: A Christian Way.*

In this speech, Obama gives a balanced view of both the greatness of America, including the idea of democracy in the Declaration of Independence and Constitution, and American racism, imperialism, and genocide. The flaw in the document, or "stain" as Obama suggests, was the "nation's original sin of slavery." Slavery divided the colonies and the 1787 Philadelphia convention until it was agreed to allow the slave trade to continue for at least twenty more years, leaving "any final resolution to future generations." The bedrock theme of Obama's speech is his conviction of the responsibility of each succeeding generation to perfect the Union started by the founding fathers. Obama resolves the twin dynamics of American empire by shifting from a focus on past and traditional greatness (the subtext of which includes racism, of course) to the perfection and completion of America's greatness at some point in the future by succeeding generations. Each generation must do its part, but the fulfillment of the ideals will only happen in the future. The source of Obama's thought about perfecting the Union is Abraham Lincoln, who championed the perfection of the nation's core ideals to be realized at some future point.

In a series of debates with Stephen Douglass in 1858, Lincoln argued that the Declaration of Independence is not a static document with fixed truths completed in the past, but rather presented Americans with ideals as maxims, goals to be strived for that guide thought and action. Douglass argued against the equality of all human beings and contended that the Declaration of Independence did not apply to blacks. In the final debate in Alton, Illinois, Lincoln refuted this claim by making equality a maxim rather than a fixed truth.[27] For Lincoln, the Declaration of Independence sets forth general truths, rules of conduct, or fundamental principles such as equality, that only could be perfected at some point in the future. Obama follows Lincoln's strategy and attempts to bridge America's racial divide.

Obama admits that the ideal of American democracy is great and remarkable and the implementation of the founding ideal of America was flawed. Obama resolves this tension by suggesting that the design

27. Lincoln-Douglass Debate, Last Joint Debate at Alton, Illinois, October 15, 1858, accessed March 17, 2017, http://www.bartleby.com/251/72.html.

of America is to perfect the Union in succeeding generations. Obama attempts to change the fixed narrative of racial discourse in America by suggesting that it is the responsibility of whites and blacks to perfect the Union rather than to focus exclusively on white or black grievances and trauma. This leads to the final idea to discuss in this Introduction: White supremacy and refusal of the challenges of equality.

White supremacy refuses to accept the challenge of equality, and thus refuses to perfect the Union. I use the phrase *white supremacy,* even though it can be incendiary, so let me briefly explain what I mean.

In the upcoming chapter 1 entitled "Race, Shrinking Whiteness, and Four Qualities of the Moral Imagination of Robert F. Kennedy," following Thomas Kane, I give a fuller explanation and discussion of my definition of white supremacy. Most Americans have a narrow and limited view of white supremacy. For them, white supremacy is reduced to individuals saying the N-word, individuals committing acts of violence physically or psychologically against persons of color, or historical attitudes and passions that have long passed, such as slavery, lynching, and the signs of a white and colored segregated Jim Crow America. With this narrow definition, it would appear to many that white supremacy is gone. Quite to the contrary, the conscious and unconscious acts, and the intentions of white supremacy are well and alive. They are covertly institutionalized, such as in systems of mass incarceration, police shooting and killing unarmed African American people, tactics of voter suppression, and the race-baiting and hatred of alt-right groups, to name a few. These institutionalized racial systems and people in the systems believe and ensure that the majority of material goods, services, and resources be reserved for persons of European descent.

For generations, many white Americans have chosen and continue to choose the comfort of apathy regarding resource inequity over the genuine challenge of equality—material, political, rhetorical, and representational. The source of this denial of equality is hotly debated and attributed as racial hostility by some and racial indifference by others. Michele Alexander defines racial indifference as "a lack of compassion and caring about race and racial groups," and defines racial hostility as the assumption that systems are "necessarily predicated on the desire to harm other racial groups."[28] Alexander posits racial indifference and the "comfort of apathy" as overarching sources of the refusal of the vast majority of white Americans to take up the challenge of equality—material, political, rhetorical, and representational. The late Derrick Bell of New York University Law School, one of the founders of Critical Race Theory and the concept of "interest convergence," made the argument that whites will not support civil rights policies that may threaten white social status. He maintained that from the beginning of America, the framers of the Constitution chose the "original sin," rewards of property over justice. Bell believed that white people would support racial justice when there is something in it for them, when there is a convergence between the interests of white people and racial justice. Bell asserted that the Supreme Court ended the longstanding policy in 1954 of "separate but equal" in *Brown v. Board of Education* as a result of the embarrassment of segregation before the world, hence the need to support civil and human rights, given the Cold War with the Soviet Union.[29] Whether the source is racial indifference, racial hostility, or a lack of interest convergence, the bottom line is white supremacy authorizes white privilege and refuses the challenge of equality in America.

The sum total of a balanced view of the American character and identity, the rituals and benefits of freedom for a few, the quest to perfect our Union, and the white supremacy refusal of equality is that the moral imagination of America in the second decade of the twenty-first century is dominated by the idolatrous and diabolical imagination. Again, what has and always will hinder the moral imagination of America is white supremacy that reserves the rights and benefits of America only to a few. The election of Donald Trump—who trumpets cynicism; white nationalism; patriarchy; ridicule of immigrants, women, and disabled persons; a Muslim ban; and the support of Trump from the KKK and alt-right racist groups—is indicative of the pervasiveness of the idolatrous and diabolical

28. Michele Alexander, *The New Jim Crow: Mass Incarceration in the Age of Colorblindness* (New York: The New Press, 2010), 203.

29. Bell is the source of Barak Obama's aforementioned use of racism as America's "original sin." The best source for an overall perspective of Bell's writings is *The Derrick Bell Reader*, ed. Richard Delegado and Jean Stefanic (New York: New York University Press, 2005).

imagination. Let me be crystal clear: racism, misogyny, cynicism, xenophobia, patriarchy, and anti-immigrant blame discourse always surges from the heart of the diabolical imagination.

The Church and Moral Imagination

Earlier in the chapter I shared how Burke suggested that the spirit of religion has long sustained moral imagination and moral imagination must be expressed afresh in each age. This means that if moral imagination in America is primarily centered on the idolatrous and diabolical imagination, we must correspondingly conclude that there is a lack of moral imagination in the religion of America, and most particularly in the contemporary American church. T. S. Elliot, in reference to morality and spirituality suggests:

> The number of people in possession of any criteria for discriminating between good and evil is very small…the number of the half-alive hungry for any form of spiritual experience, or for what offers itself as spiritual experience, high or low, good or bad is considerable. My own generation has not served them well….Woe to the foolish prophets, that follow their own spirit, and have seen nothing.[30]

Eliot's statement is true today, and therefore, is an indictment of the majority of the American Christian church. His admission that his generation has not served the people well could be spoken of the majority, but not all, of the contemporary church in the second decade of the twenty-first century. People operating in the idolatrous and diabolical imagination have a difficult time discerning good from evil and are hungry for any form of spiritual experience, high or low, good or bad. Where is the moral imagination of the church? If religion sustains moral imagination, and there is little moral imagination, how is the church functioning? What is the church doing? My belief is that the majority of the church has not served the people well.

---

30. Kirk, "The Moral Imagination."

Therefore, the purpose of this book is to clearly delineate how moral imagination can be fostered in the church through preaching. In the context of preaching, I define moral imagination as

> the ability of the preacher, intuitive or otherwise, in the midst of the chaotic experiences of human life and existence, to grasp and share God's abiding wisdom and ethical truth in order to benefit the individual and common humanity.

Moral imagination of the true Christian faith advocates against racism, misogyny, patriarchy, homophobia, discrimination, cynicism, scapegoating, blame, and so on, and visions all human beings created in the image of God, and as such, warrants the ritual and benefits of freedom for all. It is simply not possible for adherents of the Christian faith to support systems and individuals that advocate that only a few lives matter. When the church advocates and supports individuals and systems that articulate and function in such a manner, the church has abdicated its leadership in moral imagination, and then the culture and society can only slip into the human default position of idolatrous and diabolical imagination.

Preachers would do well to look at key expressions of moral imagination, inside and outside the church, to find models of the creative expression of moral imagination. To speak to the moral imagination of twenty-first-century America, there are lessons that can be learned from the chaotic 1950s and '60s, a time of some of the most important expressions of moral imagination in American history. There are moments and periods in American history where, because of moral imagination, there is significant movement to freedom, where the movement to make the reality that all lives matter visible and tangible in culture and society moves us closer to perfecting the Union. Let me explain to you how the book is organized.

The first chapter is entitled "Race, Shrinking Whiteness, and Four Qualities of the Moral Imagination of Robert F. Kennedy." This is based on a lecture that I wrote for the 2016 Academy of Homiletics meeting in San Antonio, Texas, and delivered ten days after the presidential election. The writing of this lecture generated thoughts about the moral imagination that blossomed into this book. In this chapter, I want to put the discussion of race front and center, specifically, the relationship of brown, black, and excluded white people with the phenomena of "whiteness" in America. My argument is that we need increased moral imagination to discuss and effectively deal with the perennial issue of race and whiteness, including the phenomena of shrinking whiteness. The moral imagination of Robert F. Kennedy in his famous speech on April 4, 1968, the night of the assassination of Martin Luther King Jr., is an excellent model from which we might learn qualities of the moral imagination for preaching.

In the second chapter, "A Requiem: "I'm Happy Tonight": Four Qualities of the Moral Imagination of Martin Luther King Jr.," I look at the moral imagination of Martin Luther King Jr., specifically, in his final speech/sermon, "I've Been to the Mountaintop," delivered April 3, 1968, the night before his assassination. King is a paradigmatic example of the agonizing struggle, and yet the ultimate victory, of preaching with moral imagination. I will examine the difficult and potentially chaotic exigencies surrounding King as he rose to the pulpit that night in Memphis, Tennessee. King's speech/sermon and its cosmic resolution revealed to the audience God's abiding wisdom and ethical truth. From the depths of his moral imagination, King says, "I'm happy tonight."

In chapter 3, entitled "Who Is the Moral Leader of Our Nation? Four Qualities of Moral Imagination and New Moral Leadership," I explore the potential of the four qualities of the moral imagination to offer critique and challenge to our nation that is above and beyond the normal divisions and categories of race, class, religion, gender, political labels or parties, and so on, that are based in the idolatrous and diabolical imagination. The truth of these four qualities of moral imagination can be applied to leadership in order to discern whether or not it is moral. I close the chapter by, following Dov Seidman, articulating a new vision of moral leadership based in the four qualities of the moral imagination.

In chapter 4, entitled "How to Preach a Dangerous Sermon: Four Qualities of Moral Imagination in a Sermon," I suggest a homiletical method that allows the preacher to include the four qualities of moral imagination in a sermon. Following a clear delineation of the method, I present the sermon "Did Heaven Make a Mistake?" as a tangible demonstration of preaching with the four qualities of the moral imagination in mind.

In the closing section entitled "The Final Word: The 'Freedom Faith' of Prathia L. Hall," I offer a final, powerful example, and hope to honor the life and work of Prathia L. Hall and the powerful role of women in the struggle for freedom and equality. Hall entitled the struggle for equality from her moral imagination as "Freedom Faith." There is a close interconnection between the four qualities of the moral imagination and Hall's freedom faith. Finally, I will present Hall's sermon "Freedom-Faith."

RACE AND SHRINKING WHITENESS:

FOUR QUALITIES OF THE MORAL IMAGINATION OF ROBERT F. KENNEDY

Identity politics has come to be associated with minorities and often a patronizing undercurrent as though to refer to nonwhite people motivated by an irrational herd instinct. White people have practiced identity politics since the inception of America, but it is [after the 2016 presidential election] laid bare and impossible to evade.[1]

Chimamanda Ngozi Adichie

In the introduction, I expressed the view that what has and always will hinder the moral imagination of America is the white supremacy that reserves the rights and benefits of America to only a few. I want in this chapter to put the discussion of race front and center: specifically, the relationship of brown, black, and excluded white people with the

---

1. Chimamanda Ngozi Adichie, "Now Is the Time to Talk About What We Are Actually Talking About," *The New Yorker,* December 2, 2016, http://www.newyorker.com/culture/cultural-comment/now-is-the-time-to-talk-about-what-we-are-actually-talking-about.

phenomena of "whiteness" in America.[2] Henceforth, most often, I will say race and whiteness because usually when race is discussed, it is assumed that the speaker is exclusively considering black or brown people. I will use race and whiteness to encompass all of the identity politics of America. My basic argument in this chapter is that we need increased moral imagination to discuss and effectively deal with the perennial issue of race and whiteness, including the phenomena of shrinking whiteness. The moral imagination of Robert F. Kennedy in his famous speech on April 4, 1968, the night of the assassination of Martin Luther King Jr., is an excellent model from which we might learn qualities of the moral imagination for preaching. To officially begin our discussion, even though I considered moral imagination in the introduction, I want to return to it again.

Moral imagination was coined by Edmund Burke and occurs in his *Reflections on the Revolution in France.* Burke laments the revolutionaries' disregard for moral imagination indicative of the strong and sudden changes being brought to customs and institutions of civil society. Burke said:

> All the decent drapery of life is to be rudely torn off. All of the superadded ideas, furnished from the wardrobe of a moral imagination, which the heart owns and the understanding ratifies, as necessary to cover the defects of our own naked shivering nature, and to raise it to dignity in our estimation, are to be exploded as ridiculous, absurd, and antiquated fashion.[3]

In an article titled "Defining 'Moral Imagination,'" Jonathan Jones gives a fuller explanation of the concept:

> To be a citizen is not to be an autonomous individual; it is a status given by a born existence into a world of relations to others. To be fully human is to embrace the duties and obligations toward a purpose of security and endurance for, first and foremost, the family and the local community. Suc-

---

2. I subscribe to Marla Frederick's definition of race: "Race is defined as a socially constructed category based historically on a system guaranteeing the inequitable distribution of power and economic benefit." Marla F. Frederick, *Between Sundays: Black Women and Everyday Struggles of Faith* (Berkley: University of California Press, 2003), 10.

3. See Russell Kirk, "The Moral Imagination," *The Russell Kirk Center for Cultural Renewal,* accessed August 31, 2017, http://www.kirkcenter.org/detail/the-moral-imagination/

cess is measured by the development of character, not the fleeting emotions of status. Thinking "sacramentally," (meaning humans are connected with a sacramental order of creation, a configuration of the mind in communion with the divine and beyond the rational) this is a sense that nature was created in such a manner that humans can draw "true analogies," wisdom inaccessible by scientific method.[4]

Combining this discussion of moral imagination with discussions in the introduction, I would define moral imagination as *the ability of the preacher, intuitive or otherwise, in the midst of the chaotic experiences of life and existence, to grasp and share God's abiding wisdom and ethical truth in order to benefit the individual and common humanity.* To make moral imagination come alive in our contemporary moment, I look at race, the ghetto, and public resources in America.

Race, the Ghetto, and Public Resources in America

Race and whiteness lurk within and under every aspect of American life. Race and whiteness is one of the most chaotic subjects and experiences of the American experiment, and one often wonders how much of our discussion is helpful, if we discuss it at all, given that in our media, politics, economics, and religion, there is so much heat and so very little light. How does one constructively preach about the taboo subject of race and whiteness? How does one preach beyond the extremes of Pollyanna, "kum by yah" platitudes based on scriptural truths that sound syrupy and sweet, or the condescending sacred prophetic judgments offering the common currency of blame and damnation? How do we preach to the twin dynamics of empire, the awesome release of creative energy that is America, and also the unparalleled violence and oppression? In many pulpits, we do not preach about race and whiteness at all, given its explosive potential to polarize and divide. When we do not choose productive

---

4. Jonathan Jones, "Defining 'Moral Imagination,'" *First Things*, July 1, 2009, https://www.first things.com/blogs/firstthoughts/2009/07/defining-moral-imagination.

options and constructively confront issues of race and whiteness, the issues do not go away. I have learned through experience what a teacher once taught: "buried feelings do not die." There are so many buried feelings around race and whiteness in America, and they often surface— sometimes at the most unfortunate and inopportune times—and create even more havoc by adding additional layers to the buried feelings that do not die.

America is fond of believing that the country has made significant racial progress in the last fifty years, and in many places, given the dismal and awful stations we started from, we have. What we are often not prepared for is the reality that this progress often comes as two steps forward and one step backward. While I had hoped that the presidency of Barack Obama would move us forward toward being "post-racial," the disappointing fact is that some of the responses to Obama's presidency have been the most grotesque features of whiteness, racism, and othering, such as Trump's five-year campaign of "Birtherism." Much of this— amidst other legitimate critical and important global, economic, and religious factors—has led to the rise of Donald J. Trump as president. Laced with white supremacy and white nationalism, the alt-right brand (white supremacist right) of paranoid politics, including pettiness, vindictiveness, misogyny, xenophobia, discrimination against minorities, conspiracy theories occupies the highest office in the land with Trump's presidency. And while there is much complexity in motivations for voting that led to his election, I cannot dismiss the fact that dog whistle appeals to whiteness was a major theme of his campaign. What is so dangerous is that in the successful campaign of Donald J. Trump, normal white supremacist thought, or whiteness, by many average Americans morphed with the paranoid style of the white nationalist racist fringe of America to deliver him into the White House. I did say the normal and everyday mainstream white supremacy, or whiteness, so let me explain myself.

When I suggest everyday and normal white supremacy and whiteness, I concur with Thomas Kane who, in his article "Bringing the Real: Lacan and Tupac," suggests the following:

By *white supremacist*, I don't mean to suggest that the entire nation is wearing Klan gear or painting graffiti swastikas; instead, I intend the term to connote a *de facto* white supremacy, where the privilege of whiteness is assumed and perpetuated across generations so that taking the historically long view, the majority of property, wealth, and material goods are owned and operated for white profit. This inequality is embedded in our society by generations of choosing the comfort of apathy over genuine challenge of equality—material, political, rhetorical, and representational.[5]

As I said in the introduction, most Americans are not using the N-word, and the signs of white and colored are long gone, but the conscious and unconscious acts and intentions of white supremacy, particularly in its institutionalized expressions, ensure that the majority of goods, services, and resources be owned and operated for the profit of persons of European descent. And I do mean white supremacy in its form of visible racial hostility and its hidden and passive form of racial indifference. Racial indifference is just as real and dangerous as racial hostility because it sets a complicit atmosphere for the racial hostility of white supremacy to thrive and grow. Or, as I continue to lament, racial indifference made it possible for the alt-right (white supremacist right) to occupy seats of influence at the table in the White House. The paranoid alt-right has gone from the fringe to the center of American political discourse with the complicity of racial indifference.

I opened the introduction with Langston Hughes's quotation, that "freedom is a strong seed planted in a deep need." I did not explicate what I meant by "freedom," and so let me do that now. Consistent with the aforementioned definition of white supremacy as the majority of property, wealth, and material goods owned and operated for white profit, there is a connection between the administration of public resources and freedom. Freedom could be defined as what public resources are provided to one group of people and not provided to another. Freedom is a form of privilege.

Because public resources flow to some communities in their freedom, they experience quality housing, health care services, economic

---

5. Thomas Kane, "Bringing the Real: Lacan and Tupac," *Prospects: An Annual of American Cultural Studies,* ed. Jack Salzman (New York: Cambridge University Press, 2002), 661.

development, decent insurance rates, effective policing, quality schools, public services, grocery stores, businesses, and concern by politicians. Public policy by virtue of biased laws and statutes, court decisions, lobbyists, school education decisions, policing practices, corporate licentiousness, and American civil religion ensure that the majority of the resources remain in the hands of an ever smaller group of "white" and privileged Americans.

Parenthetically, let me suggest that the concept of America as the land where any man or woman can succeed is coming under more and more assault and the factual evidence insists that it is not "rags to riches," but "rags to rags" or "riches to riches." What I am suggesting is that even some white people do not have access to "whiteness" of freedom. White privilege or whiteness is shrinking. Thomas Piketty suggests the source is what he calls "patrimonial capitalism." Piketty suggests that between 1977 and 2007, 60 percent of the total increase of the national income of our nation went to the top 1 percent.[6] This is a result of a few people, who by virtue of their wealth, can buy the political system and establish governance that primarily protects and advances their interests. It is not news to anyone that as wealth accumulates in fewer and fewer hands, the very rich have power over politics, government, and society. It has always been true that black and brown people were mostly excluded from resources, but massive inequality is indicative of the fact that whiteness is shrinking. It is not just that black lives do not matter, the fact is only a few lives matter in America. There are many white lives that do not matter. Many white lives do not have access to freedom.

My point about freedom and public resources is not clear so let me further illustrate by discussing the American concept of the "ghetto." Kane suggests that one of the sites of white supremacy is the constructed mythology of the ghetto. Our national self-image is bound up in white "simulated suburban society" and small town America. Those in many black and brown neighborhoods have been historically and materially separated from this simulated reality. Segregated into certain neighborhoods,

---

6. Thomas Piketty, *Capital in the Twenty-First Century,* trans. Arthur Goldhammer (Cambridge, MA: The Belknap Press of Harvard University Press, 2014), 297.

the media portrays as random the apparently senseless acts of violence that wear only a black or Latinx mask. The myth perpetuates the ghetto as a living nightmare, a place of violence and warfare, a jungle if you will. Racially insensitive institutions are therefore justified in profiling many blacks and Hispanics, such as in the policies and tactics as the "War on Drugs," "stop and frisk," and the immutable "law and order," resulting in the mass incarceration of many Black and Latinx people, including the regular and systemic shooting of so many unarmed African Americans. It is not only the police, but the District Attorneys, Review Boards, the procedures, laws of the land, the courts, the legislatures, and the Supreme Court that sanction so much of this white supremacy, often based upon the politics of fear, leading to racial hostility and racial indifference. It is interesting that prison stocks went up significantly after the election of Trump. Investors understood that based upon Trump's campaign rhetoric of "law and order" and "stop and frisk" that the prison population, of especially black and brown people, would go up. Now, undeniably there is the reality of gangs, the criminal element, and violence in the ghetto. It can be a tough place both to live in and to police. Citizens want effective community-based policing that serves to make neighborhoods safe and stable, not the racial profiling and shooting of unarmed black and brown men and women. The community wants input as to how they are policed and not the top-down paternalism of an imposed "law and order." People who have freedom have a voice in their policing, but often people in minority communities are not afforded this right.

Kane suggests that "the media's role seems to further inscribe the already centuries-old nativist and primitivistic view of African Americans and Hispanics perpetuated by white or white-thinking institutions."[7] Donald J. Trump fits squarely in this white supremacist way of looking at the ghetto. We can discover this white supremacist mythology by looking at the appeal of Donald J. Trump to black and Latinx voters in the 2016 presidential campaign. Trump offered his commentary on the state of African American and Latinx communities by saying that the government

---

7. Kane, 646.

had totally failed them. Claiming that the Democrats had failed in the inner cities, Trump suggested that the numbers had gotten worse:

> Poverty. Rejection. Horrible Education. No housing, no homes, no ownership. Crimes at levels that no one has ever seen...to the African Americans, who I employ so many, so many people, to the Hispanics, tremendous people: What the hell do you have to lose?[8]

As a part of Trump's commentary, he often added the reminder of the number of shooting deaths in Chicago, "President's Obama's hometown," coupled with comments about the prevalence of black-on-black crime.

There are many problems with Trump's analysis of the state of African Americans and Hispanics, such as the paternalism of when he mentions African Americans, he has to mention how many he employs. My main problem with this kind of rhetoric is it reinforces white supremacy and the mythology of white thinking institutions because it allows whites to take no responsibility for the social policy in the creation, construction, and preservation of the ghetto. America tends to assume that ghettoes just happened, often by lack of responsibility, initiative, and laziness of individuals and families. Patrick Sharkey argues that "the reality is that areas composed primarily of racial and ethnic minorities have been the object of severe disinvestment and abandonment for most of the past half century."[9] Because only a few lives matter, ghettoes are the result of the social and public policy of America well beyond the last half century that denies public resources to certain groups of people. Normal and average whiteness does not take any responsibility for ghettoes and one neighborhood having massive resources and another having virtually none.

Where suburban communities have fared well, they have had massive support from the federal government:

---

8. Jenna Johnson, "Donald Trump to African American and Hispanic Voters: 'What Do You Have to Lose?'" *Washington Post*, August 22, 2016, https://www.washingtonpost.com/news/post-politics/wp/2016/08/22/donald-trump-to-african-american-and-hispanic-voters-what-do-you-have-to-lose/?utm_term=.a9ca5a151583.

9. Patrick Sharkey, *Stuck in Place: Urban Neighborhoods and the End of Progress Toward Racial Equality* (Chicago: University of Chicago Press, 2013), 179.

Suburban prosperity, where it exists, has been facilitated by federal investment in a highway and regional transportation systems that allowed firms
and workers to relocate outside of the central city. The expansion of home
ownership in suburban American was possible because of federally backed
mortgages, and home owners continue to be the recipients of the largest
housing policy the federal government operates: the home mortgage interest deduction, which disproportionately benefits middle- and upper-
income homeowners and dwarfs any housing policy targeting low-income
populations.[10]

We could make the same argument for the present resources that make
possible re-gentrification of selected places, such as urban cores in American cities. We could also make the same argument of neglect of resources
and investment in poor areas of white America.

Trump does not mention Chicago is the most segregated city in America, and that segregation was created by white supremacy, including racist
housing policy, white flight, redlining of banks and insurance companies,
organized white neighborhood watch groups, citizen councils and other
discriminatory practices meant to keep people out of certain neighborhoods and trapped in others. Rarely is it mentioned that the ghetto was
affected like other white communities by the vast amounts of unemploy-
ment based upon regional and global economic shifts. And there is a role
for choice and personal responsibility, but often the personal responsibility
argument is meant to buttress denial of the effects of the whiteness of public policy. Sharkey argues that more often than not, the ghetto is inherited
and passed down just like wealth from generation to generation. Various
forms of inequality (lack of whiteness) is organized and clustered in social
sites like neighborhoods, schools, and political districts. Inequality and
equality are organized in space. There are many people who benefit from
the classification of "good" neighborhoods and "bad" neighborhoods, and
if you are benefitting, as I am as an African American, it is easy to take
no responsibility. Even as whiteness is shrinking, a few minorities make
it into whiteness. Some argue that whiteness is more about class and less

10. Sharkey, 181–82.

9

about race as it must be acknowledged that many poor whites experience the same disinvestment as the black neighborhoods.

Shrinking Whiteness in America

I realized before, but with even greater clarity after the presidential election, that not every white person has benefited from white supremacy, whiteness, or white privilege in the same way. There are significant numbers of white people, who just like those in the ghetto, have been left out of the resources, or whiteness. I heard civil rights activist Ruby Sales talk about whiteness in some interesting ways. In a podcast titled, "Where Does It Hurt?," she asks questions about how do we develop theology or theologies that deal with a capitalist technocracy where only a few lives matter.[11] How do we raise people up from disposability to essentiality? She asks what is the public theology that can say to the white person in Massachusetts or the forty-five-year-old person in Appalachia, who is heroin addicted because they feel their lives have no meaning, often the result of the trickle down whiteness in the world today, that their lives matter? She argues that many white people have been told their whole lives that their essence is whiteness, power, and domination, and when that no longer exists, they feel like they are dying or get caught up in the throes of death.

Her comments remind me of the study by Anne Case and Sir Angus Deaton, "Rising Morbidity and Mortality in Midlife Among White Non-Hispanic Americans in the 21st Century."[12] This published study documents significant increases in the mortality of middle-aged white non-Hispanic men and women in the United States between 1999 and 2013. According to the report, mid-life mortality rates fell in every racial and ethnic group, and those aged sixty-five and above, except for middle-aged white non-Hispanic men and women. Here is an excerpt from the report:

11. Ruby Sales, "Where Does It Hurt?" *On Being with Krista Tipett,* September 15, 2016, podcast, https://onbeing.org/programs/ruby-sales-where-does-it-hurt/.

12. Anne Case and Sir Angus Deaton, "Rising Morbidity and Mortality in Midlife among White Non-Hispanic Americans in the 21st Century," September 17, 2015, http://www.pnas.org/content/112/49/15078.full.

This increase for whites was largely accounted for by increasing death rates from drug and alcohol poisonings, suicide, and chronic liver diseases and cirrhosis. This change reversed decades of progress in mortality and was unique to the United States; no other rich country saw a similar turn-around...those with less education saw the most marked increases. Rising midlife mortality rates of white non-Hispanics were paralleled by increases in midlife morbidity. Self-reported declines in health, mental health, and ability to conduct activities of daily living, and increases in chronic pain and inability to work, as well as clinically measured deteriorations in liver function, all point to growing distress in this population.

In the attempt to locate the cause of the rising mid-life mortality and morbidity, Paul Krugman writes:

In a recent interview, Mr. Deaton suggested that middle-aged whites have "lost the narrative of their lives." That is, their economic setbacks have hit hard because they expected better. Or to put it a bit differently, we're looking at people who were raised to believe in the American Dream, and are coping badly with its failure to come true.[13]

Trump was able in the presidential election cycle to appeal directly to this audience. Their pain and frustration is at the root of his racially coded and targeted whiteness slogan "Make America Great Again." Trump repeatedly said, "America will win again," and thereby promised to restore their narrative of power and domination again. So where is the church? Where are the preachers that redefine for them what it means to be fully human outside of power and domination? Sales argues that there is a spiritual crisis in white America, a crisis of meaning. And finally, she says:

We talk a lot today about black theologies but I want a liberating white theology. I want a theology that speaks to Appalachia. I want a theology that begins to deepen people's understanding of their capacity to live fully human lives and to touch the goodness inside of them rather than call upon the part of themselves that is not relational. Because it is nothing wrong

---

13. Paul Krugman, "Despair, American Style," *New York Times*, Op-Ed, November 9, 2015, https://www.nytimes.com/2015/11/09/opinion/despair-american-style.html.

with being European American. That is not the problem. It is how you actualize that history and how you actualize that reality.[14]

I want the reader especially to hear that there is nothing wrong with being European-American, it is whether or not one adopts white supremacy. Often, when race and whiteness are discussed, the assumption is made that all European Americans reserve the rights of freedom to the European American group and are white supremacists. All European Americans are not white supremacists.

Sales wants, and I do too, a theology that gives hope and meaning to people who are struggling to have meaning in a world where they no longer are as essential to whiteness as they once were, whether they are white, black, Latinx, female, or LGBTQ. I want white and black theology that takes up the genuine challenge of equality—material, political, rhetorical, and representational. I fear that we are on the path of whiteness, domination, greed, and lust for power. And where is the church? Important constituencies of the white church are silent, for example, evangelicals, and as we found out post-election results, were supportive of Trump's power and domination narrative. Again, there are many reasons as to why a person votes for a candidate, but at the very least we can say that evangelicals said nothing to oppose the racially charged power and domination language. I consider it a failure of moral imagination.

Trump has a wonderful chance to address the issues of shrinking freedom to ensure that the excluded white, black, Hispanics, women, and others could share in the prosperity of America. Trump could be a positive force for all of the disenfranchised. But he would have to dismantle dog whistle white supremacist appeals. Like many white politicians, including the southern strategy of Richard Nixon, welfare queens of Ronald Reagan era, Willie Horton ads of the George H. W. Bush campaign, the homophobic emphasis of the George W. Bush's second election, and many others, there is the use of coded racial language to assure that they are committed to white supremacy in order to win elections. No politician will use the "N-word," and everyone is against signs of "white and colored," but everyone understands the message through racially coded language

---

14. Sales, "Where Does It Hurt?"

that get the message across and allows the candidate plausible deniability. This coded language has coddled and given incubation to the paranoid style and white supremacy that are now in the mainstream and center of American politics. Trump and many people for that matter would have to dismantle the whiteness that was essential to their success and truly believe that all lives matter. We would have to take up the genuine challenge of equality—material, political, rhetorical, and representational. Admittedly, this is a tall order indeed, but there are some who, out of their moral imagination, have done it, for example, Robert F. Kennedy.

Robert F. Kennedy's Moral Imagination

I want to suggest that we might find resources to take up the genuine challenge of equality in preaching by analyzing Robert F. Kennedy's April 4, 1968, speech, given in Indianapolis, Indiana, the night of Martin Luther King Jr.'s assassination. Kennedy's speech had a constructive discussion of race and whiteness, and my goal is to look at the means of persuasion for clues and indicators as to how we might have a fruitful discussion in our time. Though there are significant differences between the social periods of 1968 and 2016, a close reading of Kennedy's eight-minute speech will offer insights and qualities of moral imagination such that more than a few lives matter.

The relationship between the Kennedys (President John F. and Attorney General Robert F.) with the civil rights movement and Martin Luther King Jr. has been well documented. In spite of intervening on behalf of the civil rights movement, Robert F. Kennedy, on October 10, 1963, signed a request from then Director of the F.B.I., J. Edgar Hoover, to wiretap the phones of Martin Luther King Jr. Some have never been able to look beyond this signature based upon the psychological and physical damage, anchored in the ability to wiretap phones, caused by the F.B.I. to King and the civil rights movement. Despite this checkered history, and his own personal family history of affluence and privilege (whiteness), by

1968 Kennedy had established himself as a vocal advocate for civil rights, social justice, peace, and nonviolence. Kennedy had investigated poverty and hunger in Mississippi and came away from that experience with the moral indignation and resolute purpose to overcome poverty and reconcile race relations in America. By this point, in regard to the black community, Kennedy had garnered the trust of many.

After President Lyndon Johnson's declaration that he would not enter the 1968 presidential race, Kennedy decided to run. On March 28, 1968, Kennedy filed a petition for his candidacy as President in Indiana, and kicked off his campaign with a trip through South Bend on April 4. At the gymnasium of Ball State University, Muncie, Indiana, an African American student shouted a question to Kennedy: "Mr. Kennedy, I agree with your programs and proposals, but in order for them to work, you are placing a great deal of faith in White America. My question is, is this faith justified?" Kennedy responded: "Yes! There is a small minority that says black people are inferior... but the vast majority want to do the right thing."[15]

At 7:35 p.m., Kennedy, on the plane to Indianapolis, heard the news that Martin Luther King Jr. had been shot in Memphis, Tennessee. At 8:40p.m., he was informed that King had died from his wounds. The consensus of public officials in Washington and Indianapolis, including the local police, was that his scheduled Indianapolis campaign stop be cancelled. Civil Rights leader John Lewis was the countervailing voice that counseled Kennedy to continue. Kennedy made the decision to make the campaign stop.

At 8:45 p.m., the crowd gathered in Indianapolis, made up of both white and black. Some knew of the death of King and some did not. Black militants had come angry and ready to do harm to white people. As witnesses attest, they were not the only ones that were armed. While there was no way to estimate, there was also gasoline, chains, guns, and knives. There were also police rifles on rooftops for security.

---

15. "A Ripple of Hope," directed by Donald Boggs (2010), distributed by PBS Distribution, http://www.shoppbs.org/product/index.jsp?productId=3975308, DVD.

At 9:25 p.m., Kennedy pulled out yellow sheets of his quickly con-structed handwritten notes as he rose up on a flatbed truck to speak. *I have some—some very sad news for all of you … and I think, sad news for our fellow citizens and people who love peace all over the world; and that is that Martin Luther King, Jr was shot and killed tonight in Memphis, Tennessee.*[16] He announces the news and several in the audience scream in shock and disbelief. He pauses in the moment—quietly, methodically, and proceeds speaking slowly. He shifts from a campaign speech to a brief eulogy for King and a major appeal for compassion and nonviolence. *Martin Luther King dedicated his life to love and justice between fellow human beings. He died in the cause of that effort. … In this difficult time for the United States, it's perhaps well to ask what kind of a nation we are and what direction we want to move it. For those of you that are black—considering the evidence evidently is that there were white people who were responsible—you can be filled with bitterness, and with hatred, and a desire for revenge.* He calls out, names, and therefore acknowledges the simmering pain, anger, and frustration of African Americans in the crowd. He suggests that the nation has a choice to move in the direction of greater polarization, *black people amongst blacks, and whites amongst white, filled with hatred toward one an-other. Or, we can make an effort, as Martin Lither King did, to understand, and to comprehend, and replace that violence, that stain of bloodshed that has spread across our land, with an effort to understand, compassion, and love.* He returns to the theme of the potential hatred and mistrust at the injustice of the King shooting against all white people and creates identification with these feelings by announcing: *For those of you who are black and are tempted to be filled with hatred and mistrust of the injustice of such an act, against all white people, I would only say that I can also feel in my own heart this same kind of feeling. I had a member of my family, killed, but he was killed by a white man.* After this profound statement, he returns to the main theme of the speech that people in the United States had to make an effort to understand to get beyond the difficult times. He then quotes his favorite poet Aeschylus:

---

16. All quotations in italics are from Robert F. Kennedy, "Remarks on the Assassination of Martin Luther King Jr.," *American Rhetoric*, http://www.americanrhetoric.com/speeches/rfkonmlkdeath.html.

15

Even in our sleep, pain which cannot forget
falls drop by drop upon the heart,
until, in our own despair,
against our will,
comes wisdom
through the awful grace of God.

He says that the United States does not need hatred, violence, division, and lawlessness, but love, wisdom, and understanding compassion. He calls for a feeling of justice towards those who suffer in the United States whether they be white or black. The audience audibly responds with applause. He encourages them to return home and *say a prayer for the family of Martin Luther King...but more importantly say a prayer for our own country, which all of us love—a prayer for understanding and that compassion of which I spoke.* He reassures faith in the nation and makes sure that the audience knows that this is not the end of violence and lawlessness. The nation will have difficult times in the future. *We can do well in this country. We will have difficult times. We've had difficult times in the past...and we will have difficult times in the future. It is not the end of violence; it is not the end of lawlessness; and it is not the end of disorder.* He repeats the theme of his statement to the young African American student at Ball State University: *But the vast majority of white people and the vast majority of black people in this country want to live together, want to improve the quality of our life, and want justice for all human beings that abide in our land.* The audience applauds again. He closes the speech by asking the audience to dedicate themselves to what the Greeks wrote many years ago: *To tame the savageness of man and make gentle the life of this world.* Finally, he asks them to say a prayer for the country and the American people.

I am struck by the moral imagination of Robert F. Kennedy as expressed in the thoughts, content, feeling, mood, tones, of the speech. From the speech, I would like to identify four qualities of the moral imagination that must be located in the preacher before they can be translated into homiletical expression for the pew. These are the qualities from which the "stuff" of the moral imagination is constructed, the raw material of the moral imagination. What is difficult, given the limits of this chapter, is to bring these qualities into full homiletical expression. I will do this homiletical method work in chapter 4 titled, "How to Preach a Dangerous Sermon: Four Qualities of Moral Imagination in a Sermon." Let me now discuss the four qualities in Kennedy's speech, the raw materials of the moral imagination that we might seek to cultivate in ourselves and our preaching. The four qualities evidenced in Kennedy's speech are: (1) envisioned equality and represented that by his physical presence; (2) saw King's death as a catalyst or bridge to create opportunities to overcome the past and make new decisions for peace and justice; (3) found wisdom in ancient texts and sources of truth, the wisdom of the ages; and (4) addressed the audience in the language of poetry and art that lifts and elevates the human spirit by touching the emotive chords of wonder, mystery, and hope.

Four Qualities of Moral Imagination

The first quality of moral imagination was that Kennedy had the capacity to *envision equality and represent that by his physical presence.* Kennedy did not choose the comfort of apathy over the genuine challenge of equality—material, political, rhetorical, and representational. Kennedy, in his campaign, took up the challenge of equality by attempting to balance the white backlash voter and the inner city black voter, under the moral rubric of resolving poverty and race relations. Like most politicians, to handle this balance, Kennedy changed his message depending on his audience, stressing law and order with white voters and justice with inner city black voters. Some of the roots of his desire to resolve poverty and race relations was a visit to Cleveland, Mississippi, where he saw the effects of poverty—people had little food, despair, and diseases that he did not know existed in America. He saw the effects because he showed up and came out of the experience with the determination to resolve both race relations and poverty.

The most visible and tangible evidence of equality is that he moved beyond the stereotype of the ghetto as a place of violence and mayhem—a jungle, if you will. At the risk of violence, he showed up to speak in a

17

time of national calamity, the assassination of King, and communicated by his physical presence, even before his words, that he genuinely believed that all lives mattered. He severed the simulated suburban society/ghetto myth, moved out of his privileged position of whiteness, and was found in a black neighborhood the night of the death of Martin Luther King Jr. It takes moral imagination to demonstrate physical presence in times of crisis and danger. We underestimate the power of physical presence and the moral imagination that makes it a necessity that one shows up. Showing up creates the opportunity for empathy and understanding. The preacher that preaches with moral imagination must show up, not just for a photo op, but as the result of a moral imagination of equality, genuine empathy, and compassion for the people, whether they be white, black, immigrant, LGBTQ, or any member of the human family.

The second quality of moral imagination was that he saw *empathy as a catalyst or bridge to create opportunities to overcome the past and make new decisions for peace and justice.* In the midst of crisis, he believed through empathy, that is, the ability to understand, comprehend, and love were resources for new community. He had the moral imagination to harness the challenge that King's death was a significant opportunity for all to see their common humanity and create a better community. Where some see violence, disruption, revenge, fear, mistrust, and hatred, he saw an opportunity for new community.

Indicative of his empathy, one of the most gripping moments in the speech was the mention of his brother's death. After stating that the evidence was that King was killed by a white man, he communicated that he understood how blacks could be upset and would want to do violence and harm to white people. He says that he had those same feelings because his brother was killed by a white man. He communicated with them at the level of grief, that is, the common experience of losing someone that you love deeply, something common to us all. He lost his brother and they lost theirs. He conceived, in his moral imagination, empathy as an opportunity to understand and comprehend.

This speech was the first time that he ever addressed his brother's death in public. He was wearing his brother Jack's coat when he gave the speech.

I will return to this at the end, but based upon his own experience of grief and loss, he could see empathy as a catalyst or bridge for new decisions for equality because maybe in common empathy we could discover that all lives are human, and all lives matter.

Thirdly, preachers who would grapple with moral imagination must find *wisdom in ancient texts, sources of ancient wisdom and truth, the wisdom of the ages.* The primary source of the wisdom of the ages for me is the Christian Bible. Sources say that when Kennedy's brother was killed, he, as a Catholic, had a crisis of faith. The night of his brother's death, he was heard to cry out, "Why God?" Those close to him say that he lost his faith. He struggled greatly and wrestled with blaming himself for his brother's death given his work in the assassination plot on Fidel Castro in Cuba, and his relentless work against the Mafia. The very afternoon of his brother's death, he called the Mafia and asked if they had they killed his brother. They said they had not.

From his reading in Greek mythology, he concluded that pride and arrogance would result in payback from the gods. Foolish pride and dangerous overconfidence challenge the gods, and bring about human downfall. He considered that the Kennedys had overreached with pride and arrogance, and his brother's death was the gods taking retribution on the family. In the Greeks, he saw clearly that the great fall of humankind is pride and arrogance.

In that context, he found great hope in a quote from Aeschylus and quoted it to the crowd:

> Even in our sleep, pain which cannot forget...comes wisdom through the awful grace of God.

He concluded that suffering produces wisdom. This suffering, this death of King, like the death of his brother, could produce great wisdom through the awful grace of God. His source of wisdom was the Greeks. The preacher that grapples with moral imagination must connect with the wisdom of the ages. The primary source of the wisdom of the ages for me is the Christian Bible. I acknowledge that there are many sources of the wisdom of the ages in many religions and faiths, such as Judaism, Buddhism, Islam, and so on.

Fourthly, *Kennedy addressed the audience in the language of poetry and art that lifts and elevates the human spirit by touching the emotive chords of wonder, mystery, and hope.* While this is a risky proposition, it might be safe to assume that the majority of the crowd probably never heard of Aeschylus. How was this quote able to be effective? In my opinion, it is not whether they intellectually know it, but whether they can emotively understand and feel it when it is quoted. I will talk about this more in the chapter where we discuss in depth, the wisdom of the ages. As in all good preaching, he did not ignore their intellects, but reached their intellects through their hearts. You will remember from the introduction that while it is assumed that human beings understand the world through calculations and logical syllogisms, the reality is that people understand the world through images, myths, stories, and thereby comprehend relationship to God, nature, self, and others. Kirk thought that imagination ruled the world because, in his estimation, moral imagination touches the emotive chords of wonder, mystery, and hope. Through empathy, Kennedy touched these emotive chords, and it facilitated their hearing of the deeper meaning and their experience of wonder, mystery, and hope. Therefore, it did not matter that they had never heard it before. He deeply identified with their anger, suffering, and pain and was therefore able to translate this quote at the emotive level to the depths of their souls.

The implication of imagination and the emotive touching of wonder, hope, and mystery, is summed up in two quotes from a video documentary of Kennedy's campaign stop in Indianapolis that are worthy of our attention. Both quotes are in response to Kennedy quoting Aeschylus to a crowd that the documentary agrees was not familiar with the Greek poet. The first is from Professor Karl W. Anatol: "Good poetry and good art, in any context, tends to elevate." The second is by Adam Walinsky, principal speech writer for Robert Kennedy: "There is almost no person, no matter how mean their circumstances, no matter how scant their education, who cannot be addressed in the noblest terms of which the human heart is capable."[17] He addressed the audience in the noblest of terms in the human heart and moral imagination, wonder, mystery, and hope. The preacher, especially in times of chaotic experience must have the moral imagination speak to the noblest and best of the human spirit.

The conclusion to the matter of the speech on the night of April 4, 1968, was that Indianapolis did not riot. Riots occurred in seventy-six cities, forty-six people were killed, two thousand injured, and twenty-eight thousand jailed. There has not been produced scientific research to definitely prove the speech was the source of the lack of rioting. Many have anecdotally concluded that it was so.[18]

Concluding Thoughts

Finally, I am left with this question: What is it going to take to overcome America's original sin of racism? I want to go back to Kennedy's concept of empathy as a catalyst or bridge to overcome the past and make new decisions for peace and justice. While I am not a prophet of doom, my belief is that it is going to take a great deal of common death to break past the racial divisions in our culture to allow a window for genuine empathy. Kennedy saw King's death as an opportunity to overcome division and injustice. What kind of death will provide the window that we need to bridge the racial divide, economic inequality, and all the terrible divisions that we saw front and center in the presidential election, and looks like will continue into the foreseeable future? We are the most diverse nation on earth and that makes the American experiment unusually beautiful and extraordinarily tense. What will it take to overcome division?

The twentieth century had World War I, the Great Depression, World War II, and the twenty-first century had the Great Recession, but what will it take? Could you imagine some massive climate-based disaster?

---

17. "A Ripple of Hope," directed by Donald Boggs (Covenant Productions, 2008).

18. It is important to note an alternative reading of the speech as "the rhetoric of control"—see Karl W. Anatol and John R. Bittner, *Today's Speech*, vol. 16, no. 3: 31–34 and "'A Time of Shame and Sorrow': Robert F. Kennedy and the American Jeremiad," *Quarterly Journal of Speech*, vol. 76, no. 4, 1990: 401–14.

Some strain of disease that kills vast numbers of people? What about some form of dirty bomb or nuclear warhead? What about the advent of World War III? What will it take to create the window of empathy sufficient to overcome past divisions? Will we take advantage of the window once it happens upon us? Will the vast number of deaths be God's judgment for our pride and arrogance? Lincoln certainly thought that the Civil War was God's punishment for slavery. In the midst of the chaotic experience, preachers must rise and have the capacity and moral imagination to find God's truth and ethical wisdom. Russell Kirk says, "We become what others, in a voice of authority, tells us we are or ought to be," what our leaders imagine us to be.[19] I pray that our preachers and leaders will lead out of moral imagination to benefit individual and common humanity. Let's look now at the moral imagination of Martin Luther King Jr.

---

19. Fennell, "What Is Moral Imagination?" *The Imaginative Conservative*, April 11, 2016, http://www.theimaginativeconservative.org/2016/04/what-is-the-moral-imagination.html.

Chapter Two

A REQUIEM— "I'M HAPPY TONIGHT":

FOUR QUALITIES OF THE MORAL IMAGINATION OF MARTIN LUTHER KING JR.

For it was to restore the beloved community, so that the children of the world might have a legacy of peace, that he came down out of the academy, down from his pulpit, and marched his way to glory.

Stephen B. Oates

In the last chapter, I explored the speech of Robert F. Kennedy the night of the assassination of Martin Luther King Jr. and extrapolated several qualities of the moral imagination: (1) Kennedy envisioned equality and represented that by his physical presence; (2) he saw King's death as a catalyst or bridge to create opportunities to overcome the past and make new decisions for peace and justice; (3) he found wisdom in ancient texts and sources of truth; and (4) he addressed the audience in the language of poetry and art that lifts and elevates the human spirit by touching the emotive chords of wonder, mystery, and hope. Kennedy believed that it was in the power of human choice and moral action to bring about equality and freedom. In the speech the night of King's death, Kennedy anchored this belief in his faith in the cultural myth of America, the American Dream, and the ancient wisdom of the Greeks, which functioned for him as a sacred text.

I want to look now at the moral imagination of Martin Luther King Jr., specifically, in his final speech/sermon, "I've Been to the Mountaintop," delivered at Mason Temple, Memphis, Tennessee, on April 3, 1968, the night before his death. As preachers seeking to preach moral imagination, King is a paradigmatic example of the agonizing struggle, and yet ultimate beauty, healing, and victory of such preaching. It is important to remember my definition of moral imagination in the context of preaching: *Moral imagination is the ability of the preacher, intuitive or otherwise, in the midst of the chaotic experiences of human life and existence, to grasp and share God's abiding wisdom and ethical truth in order to benefit the individual and common humanity.* I want to look at the difficult and potentially chaotic exigencies surrounding King as he rose to the pulpit at Mason Temple that night in Memphis. King's speech/sermon and its cosmic resolution revealed to the audience God's abiding wisdom and ethical truth. From the depths of his moral imagination, King says, "I'm happy tonight."

Since this is a book on preaching and we are talking about moral imagination and preaching, it is appropriate to briefly discuss King's definition of preaching in the context of "I've Been to the Mountaintop." There is a particular point in the speech/sermon that I will discuss later in the close reading of the speech/sermon that King says to the audience in Memphis that he is always "happy" to see a relevant ministry. When King says relevant ministry, he means that preachers must follow God's commands to be concerned with the poor, slums, and social conditions such as children who cannot eat three meals a day. King says preachers can talk about the heavenly city of the "New Jerusalem," that is, "pie-in-the-sky religion," but the issue is what preachers have to say about the "new New York" or the "new Atlanta?" King is implying that every preacher functions as a prophet in the tradition of Jeremiah and Amos. Keith Miller suggests this, in his excellent book on the "I've Been to the Mountaintop" speech, *Martin Luther King's Biblical Epic: His Final, Great Speech*:

> King's evocation of scriptural calls to prophecy is the cornerstone of his defi-nition of preaching or, possibly, *is* his definition of preaching—a message especially salient for the numerous homilists listening at Mason Temple.[1]

King mentions several Memphis preachers by name for supporting the prophetic work of the rights of Sanitation workers and implies to every preacher and audience member that relevant preaching must speak to the needs of those denied freedom and equality. I am implying by the writing of this book and chapter that every preacher must engage in prophetic preaching, and if the term prophetic preaching is bothersome, I believe that every preacher must engage in preaching from the moral imagina-tion. Let me describe the exigencies of the rhetorical situation.

The Exigencies of the Rhetorical Situation

In discussing the exigencies of the rhetorical situation, it is possible to demarcate King's preaching and public ministry into two distinct eras of moral imagination. The first era was 1954–1965 when King expressed a buoyant optimism and hope in the positive dynamic of the cultural myth of America (i.e., personal initiative, industry, confidence, idealism, and hope) and the humane moral ethic of the Judeo-Christian tradition (i.e., justice, peace, mercy, and love). King extolled the Declaration of Independence, the Constitution, and the Hebrew prophets and Jesus, as the ultimate source of authority and inspiration to resolve the unfulfilled values of freedom and equality in America. The height of this buoyant optimism is expressed in King's 1963 "I Have a Dream" speech from the steps of the Lincoln Memorial, and the 1965 speech "Our God is March-ing On" at the conclusion of the bloody march from the Edmund Pettus

---

1. Keith D. Miller, *Martin Luther King's Biblical Epic: His Final, Great Speech* (Jackson: University of Mississippi Press, 2012), 97.

Bridge in Selma, Alabama, to the state capitol building in Montgomery, the "Cradle of Confederacy."

After 1965, until his death in 1968, the second era of King's moral imagination, King was engaged in a fundamental critique of American identity and values, and rather than resolving unfulfilled American values, King calls for "a revolution of values." In his "Beyond Vietnam" speech on April 3, 1967, at the Riverside Church in New York City, King argues that America is morally culpable in Vietnam and indicates that the culpability is related not to unfulfilled values, but to structural flaws in the American system. King directly challenges the imperial, violent, and oppressive dynamic of the cultural myth of America. According to King, as long as America is more interested in profits than people, "the giant triplets of racism, extreme materialism, and militarism are incapable of being conquered."[2] The fact that the tragic Vietnam War siphoned needed resources from President Lyndon Johnson's "War on Poverty," along with the entrenched poverty, discrimination, economic exploitation, racism, and hatred of blacks King encountered as his movement moved north, helped to ensure that King could no longer sustain the idealism and buoyant optimism of the positive dynamics of the cultural myth of America articulated from 1954–1965. King moved away from belief in human fulfillment of the basic values of the American Dream.

As a result of this post-1965 shift in belief, evidenced in almost universal condemnation of his "Beyond Vietnam" speech, King was positioned by America as a radically alienated social prophet and moved to the fringe of American political discourse. Outside of the people in the Riverside Church, most of the public reaction to "Beyond Vietnam" was condemnation. The vast majority of the press, the civil rights establishment, mainstream America, and many African Americans criticized King for demanding immediate unilateral withdrawal from Vietnam. The American public generally thought King lacked the authority to be heard on Vietnam. From their perspective, King was a preacher and civil rights advocate who should stick to civil rights and religion and stay out of international

---

2. Martin Luther King Jr., "Beyond Vietnam," *King Encyclopedia*, http://kingencyclopedia.stanford.edu/encyclopedia/documentsentry/doc_beyond_vietnam/.

affairs, about which they presumed he knew nothing. And if he did know anything, they held that he certainly could not know more than the President Lyndon Johnson and the American government.

Alongside being criticized for his position on Vietnam, another exigency was whether nonviolence was the most effective method to bring change in America. Many young black people rejected the courage and patience displayed by King and the nonviolent response to injustice in American society and advocated for more radical measures, heavily influenced by Malcolm X. The 1965 assassination of Malcolm X, coupled with the urban uprisings of 1964 and 1965, fueled the Black Power movement. In June of 1966, James Meredith walked a one-man march against fear and was shot. Many civil rights workers committed to finishing the march in Meredith's name. As they gathered in Greenwood, Mississippi, Carmichael delivered these words that were heard throughout America and around the world: "Black Power."[3] Carmichael meant to push King and the entire civil rights establishment to a more radical response to the violence and hate of America. By 1968, Black Power was a recognizable movement with a growing number of adherents. Many saw King on the defensive in regards to the strategy of nonviolent resistance in the black community.

At the request of James Lawson, King and his staff came to Memphis, Tennessee, to help the sanitation workers, hoping to revive the spirit and tone of nonviolent victories, such as 1963 in Birmingham, and prove once again the value of the strategy of nonviolence. A march was organized on March 28, 1968, in support of the sanitation workers. City officials of Memphis estimated that twenty-two thousand students skipped school to participate. King arrived late and found that the massive crowd was disorganized and on the edge of chaos. Violence broke out in the back of the march, King called off the demonstration, and King was taken away from the march for safety. Lawson told the mass of people to turn around and go back to the Clayborn Temple church. In the chaos that followed, downtown shops were looted, and a sixteen-year-old was shot and killed

---

3. Stokely Carmichael, "'Black Power' Speech, July 28, 1966," Encyclopedia.com, http://www.encyclopedia.com/history/dictionaries-thesauruses-pictures-and-press-releases/black-power-speech-28-july-1966-stokely-carmichael.

by a policeman. Police followed demonstrators back to the Clayborn Temple, entered the church, released tear gas inside the sanctuary, and clubbed people as they lay on the floor to get fresh air. A dejected King met the media to defend nonviolence, and another march was announced for April 5. It was this march that brought King to Memphis on April 4, 1968, the night of his death.

Not only was King a radically alienated social prophet, and on the defensive in regards to nonviolence, he also lived every day with an internal exigency of an increasing fear of death. King lived with the fear of death from the first bombing of his house in January 1954 to the night of his assassination in Memphis. Not only King, but also his staff, his wife, and family lived with and tried to come to terms with the many and varied death threats across the years. It is important to realize that many of the threats were not exaggerations, there were people who wanted King dead, and King's sense of apprehension was accurate and real. Historian Stephen Oates reports on King's deep forebodings:

> By 1968, the FBI had logged assassination threats against him, and the Klan amid other hate groups had him targeted for violence. With the announcement of the Poor People's Campaign, right-leaning businessmen across the land viewed him as a fiendish black devil out to wreck capitalism and establish a Communist social order that would ring the bells of doom for free enterprise, white supremacy, and their own personal wealth. Such people hated King, cursed his cause, and wished him dead. In the St. Louis area, a couple of aging right-wingers, both active in Wallace's American Independent party and supporters of Wallace for president, plotted to have King murdered. John Kauffman, a motel operator with a criminal record, had a standing offer of $20,000 to $30,000 for anybody who would kill "the big nigger." His friend John Sutherland, a St. Louis patent attorney given to wearing a confederate colonel's hat and decorating his study with Confederate flags, had put up $50,000 for King's head.[4]

Oates reports that King knew nothing about any specific contracts against his life, but was aware that the Poor People's Campaign increased the chances of his being killed. In 1968, the staff had the sense he was being

---

4. Stephen Oates, *Let the Trumpet Sound: A Life of Martin Luther King Jr.* (New York: Plume Books, 1982), 454–56.

stalked and were especially wary, given how easily John F. Kennedy was killed. According to Oates, one staffer thought "the strain of wondering when it was coming was almost overpowering." Only when King was someplace where he couldn't be shot—such as in a room without windows—could he relax with his aides and be "the Martin Luther King of the early days." In public, there was "almost a learned response to let his eyes wander and gaze," the staffer said. "It was an unconscious response. He was looking, cautious, and uncomfortable."[5]

King, in the last year of his life, grappled deeply and publicly with his own death. In several speeches, he openly and viscerally talked about his death, such as in the February 4, 1968, sermon "The Drum Major Instinct," where King concluded the sermon by imaging his own funeral. Lischer sees the speech as a "tortured farewell from one who is obsessed by thoughts of his own death and has come home one last time to 'make testimony.'"[6] In "I've Been to the Mountaintop," King openly wrestled with the fear of death. One of the prime rhetorical strategies for resolution was the adoption of biblical typology through the persona of Moses. Before the important discussion of King's strategy of biblical typology, I want to look at the specific exigencies of Memphis itself.

Joseph W. Wenzel in his article, "'A Dangerous Unselfishness:' Martin Luther King Jr.'s Speech at Memphis, April 3, 1968: A Response to Osborn," argues that when King mounted the pulpit at Mason Temple, the night before his death, he had significant challenges and much to accomplish.[7] King faced an audience full of doubts about whether it was worthwhile to continue the struggle in such a hopeless situation, given the reality of the intransigence of Mayor Loeb and the fact that the last march, on March 28, 1968, for the Memphis sanitation workers had turned violent. From Wenzel's perspective, King had to "prove" or address the following five points:

---

5. Ibid., 455–56.

6. Lischer, 107.

7. Joseph W. Wenzel, "'A Dangerous Unselfishness:' Martin Luther King Jr.'s Speech at Memphis, April 3, 1968: A Response to Osborn," in *Texts in Context: Critical Dialogues on Significant Episodes in American Political Rhetoric*, ed. Michael C. Leff and Fred C. Kauffeld (Davis, CA: Hermagoras Press, 1989), 167–80.

1. The struggle of the sanitation workers was well worth the effort, because it is part of the world-wide struggle for freedom.
2. The struggle can be won and it would be a tragedy to stop.
3. The way to win is through nonviolent demonstration and economic boycott.
4. He was not afraid and Memphis blacks should not be afraid.
5. Each individual must be selflessly committed to the struggle.

Though contextualized in Memphis, these five points are the exigencies, in one way or another, that King had to grapple with in almost every speech and in every place there was a freedom struggle in King's public career, all the way from Montgomery, Alabama, in 1954 to Memphis, Tennessee, in 1968. The speech/sermon crafted by King at Mason Temple, on a very rainy and windy night, was a response to these exigencies in Memphis, and was the last speech/sermon of King's life.

King discovered that in dealing with the violent and oppressive side of the cultural myth of America, the American audience had a difficult time with the premise that America is morally corrupt and any rhetoric, true or not, that questioned the fundamental goodness of America. Tremendous pressure was exerted on King, from both the President and the American public, the black community on Black Power, perceptions of the ineffectiveness of civil rights movement moving north, accurate fear of his own death, and the psychological warfare perpetrated upon him by J. Edgar Hoover and the FBI. I want to briefly recount an example of the warfare of the FBI upon King.

FBI director J. Edgar Hoover believed King to be a threat to national security and the most dangerous radical in America. Hoover's FBI conducted COINTELPRO, as an aggressive counterintelligence program to "destroy King's and other Black, radical, Communists, and 'Left' leaders' reputation and influence."[8] Stewart Burns records an example of the

---

8.   Gerald McKnight, *The Last Crusade: Martin Luther King, Jr., the FBI, and the Poor People's Campaign* (Boulder: Westview Press, 1998), 2.

tactics used by the FBI and their effect upon King. Though King did not visit fellow protesters behind bars, he visited Joan Baez and her mentor Ira Sandperl at the Santa Rita jail, east of San Francisco Bay on January 14, 1968. King was despondent about the fact that black hate groups were phoning him and writing him and threatening his life. Burns reports that King said to Sandperl:

> 'I shouldn't feel any different,' he confessed, than he did about white groups who had been plotting to kill him for eleven years. 'I do feel differently,' he said plaintively to his friend. 'I am really annoyed at myself. I can't believe that these black groups are people who really want my death.'[9]

The hate mail and threats did not come from black hate groups, they were the fabrications of the FBI, and as Burns says, "Hoover's men were hell-bent on torturing his soul."[10] Based upon wiretaps, "bugs," and files revealing other illegal and punitive intrusions into King's life and work, estimates reveal that the FBI's intelligence file on King was over one million pages.[11] Indeed, King was the most hounded and harassed American citizen in the history of the republic. While it is very difficult to assess the overall impact of FBI harassment of King, it was monumental, given the FBI's ability to influence newspaper articles, editorials, and disseminate negative information about King across diverse locations, including the President's desk and local newspapers.

King resolved these exigencies by a cosmic and eschatological appeal and claim that God would resolve, in God's eschatological time, all exigencies of the moral order. King had virtually given up on human choice and human behavior to bring about the moral order of freedom and equality. In his moral imagination, only a cosmic resolution from God would establish freedom and equality, a form of biblical eschatology. Racism, materialism, and militarism would not win because God would bring the people to "the promised land."

---

9. Stewart Burns, *To the Mountaintop: Martin Luther King Jr.'s Mission to Save America: 1955–1968* (New York: HarperCollins, 2004), 376–78.

10. Ibid., 378

11. Gerald McKnight, *The Last Crusade*, 6.

Fredrik Sunnemark, in his study *Ring Out Freedom: The Voice of Martin Luther King, Jr. and the Making of the Civil Rights Movement*, identifies the threefold signification structure of King's speeches and sermons as religious, idealistic, and materialistic. Because his faith was the highest rung on the signification ladder, God is the guarantor that evil will never win at the cosmic level or at the material level in the segregationist struggle against freedom. The more the alienated King is pessimistic and despairing about the status of freedom according to idealistic human choice in the material reality, the more he turns to cosmic resolution. As King loses faith in the idealistic human order to right wrongs and injustices, he turns to God's victory in the cosmic order. The last paragraph in "I've Been to the Mountaintop" is the signal declaration of God's cosmic victory in the face of the dire straits of human choice.

It is critical to understand how King actualized the victory of the cosmic struggle. Throughout his public ministry, King assumed a variety of religious personae, (i.e., Moses, the Apostle Paul, Martin Luther, the suffering servant of Hebrew scriptures, the good Samaritan, and Jesus).[12] In this speech, King chooses the persona of the Hebrew prophet Moses through biblical typology. The concept of biblical typology is a critical interpretative category to illumine King's discourse of cosmic resolution in the "I've Been to the Mountaintop" speech.

The Strategy of Biblical Typology

Since the forced migration of Africans to America and their introduction to the Christian religion, historically, the dominant trope of the African American experience has been the biblical exodus-promised-land narrative. While the imagery of the promised land and the proverbial "city set on a hill" has been a significant part of the Anglo-American narrative of the American Dream, African Americans uniquely appropriated the exodus portion of the exodus-promised-land narrative based upon their experience as an enslaved and oppressed people. For many African

---

12. Richard Lischer, "The Word That Moves: The Preaching of Martin Luther King, Jr.," *Theology Today* 46, no. 2 (July 1989): 181.

Americans, just as God called Moses to go to Pharaoh and demand "Let my people go!" likewise, God raised others like Moses to go to the American pharaoh and say, "Let my people go!" African American religious experience adopted other images and narratives from the Bible, such as the prophets, and especially Jesus Christ who was unjustly beaten, made to suffer, and was crucified (lynched), but was victorious in the resurrection. In addition to Jesus and the prophets, Moses became a mythic and symbolic figure in African American life. Zora Neale Hurston in *Moses, Man of the Mountain*, wrote "Africa has her mouth on Moses." Hurston says, "Wherever the children of Africa have been scattered by slavery, there is the acceptance of Moses as the fountain of mystic powers."[13] Poets, preachers, singers, writers, musicians, dancers, and many in the African American community adopted Moses and the exodus-promised-land narrative as a prism through which to view the African American experience.

King operated within the scope of this African American narrative for much of his public ministry. While King was hesitant to claim the Moses mantle directly, white journalists began to designate King as the black Moses, and Ralph Abernathy and others within the civil rights movement, particularly those closest to him, referred to King as the biblical Moses. Ralph Abernathy once introduced him at a Birmingham rally as, "He is the leader! He is the Moses."[14] Scott W. Hoffman discusses King as Moses when he says:

> Both the black and white presses were quick to pick up on the Moses persona, and it became a common metaphor for King the rest of his life. As early as June, 1956, *American Negro* magazine published an article entitled "Rev. M. L. King: Alabama Moses."...When *Time* declared him their 1963 Man of the Year, it quoted an "ecstatic" letter describing King as a "Moses, sent to lead his people to the Promised Land of first-class citizenship."[15]

13. Zora Neale Hurston, *Moses, Man of the Mountain* (1939; rpt. New York: Harper Perennial, 1991), xxiii–xxiv.

14. Scott W. Hoffman, "Holy Martin: The Overlooked Canonization of Dr. Martin Luther King, Jr." *Religion and American Culture: A Journal of Interpretation* 10, no. 2 (Summer 2000): 129.

15. Ibid.

Indicative of the importance of King's adoption of the mantle of Moses, King uses the exodus narrative in "I've Been to the Mountaintop" to offer hope in Memphis. Thomas Rosteck, in his article, "Narrative in Martin Luther King's 'I've Been to the Mountaintop,'" argues that King "draws increasingly upon the system of imagery associated with the story of the Biblical Exodus to define and resolve the political situation in Memphis."[16] King freely intertwines the biblical exodus and the strike in Memphis:

> You know, whenever Pharaoh wanted to prolong the period of slavery in Egypt, he had a favorite formula for doing it. . . . He kept the slaves fighting among themselves. But whenever the slaves get together, something happens in Pharaohs' court, and he cannot hold the slaves in slavery. When the slaves get together, that's the beginning of getting out of slavery. Now let us maintain unity.

On this last night in Memphis, in the very last paragraph of the speech, King becomes Moses; he performs and embodies Moses. He adopts the mantle of Moses and defines his experience and that of his audience through the eyes of Moses. I want to turn now to a close reading of "I've Been to the Mountaintop."

A Close Reading of "I've Been to the Mountaintop" [17]

The "I've Been to the Mountaintop" speech/sermon has five movements that conclude with King's masterful performance of Moses in the

16.   Thomas Rosteck, "Narrative in Martin Luther King's 'I've Been to the Mountaintop,'" *Southern Communication Journal* 58.1 (1992): 22.

17.   Martin Luther King Jr. gave no title to the last speech of his life the night of April 3, 1968. James M. Washington, in one of the first collections of the speeches of King, labels the speech as "I See the Promised Land," a quotation from the last paragraph of the speech (James M. Washington, *A Testament of Hope: The Essential Writings of Martin Luther King, Jr.* [San Francisco: Harper & Row Publishers, 1986]). The title "I've Been to the Mountaintop," also a quotation in the last paragraph of the speech, has been selected by the Martin Luther King Jr. Papers Project at Stanford University (Martin Luther King, Jr., "I've Been to the Mountaintop," *The Martin Luther King Jr. Papers Project*, https://kinginstitute.stanford.edu /encyclopedia/ive-been-mountaintop, accessed 10/12/17). Based upon the Papers Project, I have chosen "I've Been to the Mountaintop" as the title of the speech.

exodus-promised-land narrative. In reading the speech/sermon, I was struck by the number of times King mentions being "happy." I argue that the speech can be interpreted through the hermeneutical lens of "happy," when happiness is defined as the cosmic resolution of King's external and internal exigencies that we discussed in the last section. There are five critical mentions of "happy," and I have shaped a movement of the speech around each occurrence.[18] At the end of the first movement King says: "And I'm happy that he [God] has allowed me to be in Memphis." In the middle of the second movement, he says, "And I'm always happy to see a relevant ministry." At the end of the third movement, he makes a slight variation and says, "And I want to thank God once more, for allowing me to be here with you." In the fourth movement, in the story of his 1957 assassination attempt, he says: "I want to say tonight that I too am happy that I did not sneeze." Then the final and concluding movement ends with, "And so I'm happy tonight. I'm not worried about anything." Based upon concurring theme of "happy," I conclude that the speech/sermon articulates the cosmic resolution of King's moral imagination. King, in the face of his recognition of a fundamentally flawed America, loses faith in the totality of human action and choice to bring about the moral order of freedom and equality, yet does not drop out, give up, or become cynical, but continues to preach positive solutions, even if those eschatological solutions are left to God.

Movement One: "I'm happy that He's [God has] allowed me to be in Memphis."

The first and opening movement builds rapport with the audience and can be summed up in its last line: "I'm happy that He's [God has] allowed me to be in Memphis."[19] After acknowledging Ralph Abernathy for his generous introduction and admitting that he was "the best friend that he had in the world," King announces that "something is happening

---

18. Martin Luther King Jr., "I've Been to the Mountaintop," *American Rhetoric*, February 7, 2017, http://www.americanrhetoric.com/speeches/mlkivebeentothemountaintop.htm.

19. Ibid., 2.

in our world."[20] He then takes us on a trip all the way to the beginning of time, and we gain a panoramic view of all of human history. The more pessimistic King becomes in terms of humans making the right choices of change, the more King invests in the cosmic victory of God. The speech does not start out in Memphis or Birmingham or Selma, it starts out in the cosmic order, indicative of God's cosmic victory, which might indicate King's acute lack of confidence in human choice. Because faith is the highest rung on the signification ladder in King's discourse, in the opening lines of the speech, we are already being assured that the moral, spiritual, and idealistic would win.

Indicative of cosmic victory, the Almighty turns to King and says, "Martin Luther King, which age would you like to live in?"[21] King responds to God's question and takes anaphoric flight:

> I would take my mental flight by Egypt and I would watch God's children in their magnificent trek from the dark dungeons of Egypt through, or rather across the Red Sea, through the wilderness on toward the Promised Land. And in spite of its magnificence, I wouldn't stop there.[22]

King goes by the great monuments of Western Civilization: Greece, the Roman Empire, and the great Protestant Reformation where Martin Luther nailed the Ninety-Five Theses on the door of the church at Wittenburg, but each time he says, "But I wouldn't stop there." King watches Lincoln vacillate on signing the Emancipation Proclamation, sees Roosevelt grapple with the bankruptcy of America, and he says again, "But I wouldn't stop there." King remarks to God that he would be "happy" to live in the second half of the twentieth century.

King indicates that wanting to live in the second half of the twentieth century seems strange because "the world is messed up, the nation is sick, trouble is in the land, and confusion is all around." But from the cosmic vantage point, King can see that God is working in the world, and people are responding to God's work. Earlier he said "Something is happening

---

20. Ibid., 1.

21. Ibid.

22. Ibid.

in our world," and he now defines what that something is: The masses of people are rising up—Johannesburg, South Africa; Nairobi, Kenya; Accra, Ghana; and New York, Atlanta, and Memphis—the cry is the same, "We want to be free." King connects Memphis to the worldwide struggle of people of color for freedom and views these struggles from the vantage point of cosmic victory that was established by God outside of human time.

King lists two other reasons why he is "happy" to be born in the second half of the twentieth century: First, human beings are going to have to truly struggle with war and peace because we have the weaponry to destroy the world and this potentiality demands that we "grapple" with war and peace. Because of the massive weapons, the choice is nonviolence and nonexistence. If the human choice is violence, then we choose nonexistence. Secondly, according to King, the world is going to have to grapple with bringing the colored peoples of the world out of their long years of poverty. If the world does nothing, then King prophesies that the world is doomed. But despite all of this, King is happy that God has allowed him to live in the twentieth century to see freedom unfolding and happy that God has allowed him to be in Memphis.

The totality of this first movement builds positive rapport between audience and preacher. King seals this rapport by indicating how happy he is to be in Memphis. By asking God to place him in the second half of the twentieth century, King *chose* to be in Memphis. King is "happy" to be in Memphis and the audience is happy to have him there.

Movement Two: "Happy to see a relevant ministry."

The second movement involves King's explanation of the protest movement, his encouragement and inspiration to continue the struggle, as well as some practical tips to win the struggle. King explains that they are not engaged in any negative protest and arguments; that those in the movement are determined to be people and as God's children they do not have to live as they are forced to live.

King encourages the protesters to maintain unity because Pharaoh's only weapon is to keep slaves fighting amongst themselves. King suggests that they must march again to keep the focus of the issue on injustice and not on the violence that happened in the first Memphis march. King maintains that the press wants to focus on the violence, but the real issue is that thirteen hundred sanitation workers were on strike, and Memphis is not being fair to them, and suggests that mace or injunctions are not going to turn the movement around. Recalling the struggle against Bull Connor in Birmingham, King notes that the movement was not stopped by the various tactics, like water hoses and dogs. King celebrates the support of Memphis preachers like James Lawson, Billy Kyles, Ralph Jackson, and others. He only mentions a few and thanks them all and tells them "I'm always happy to see a relevant ministry," and defines a relevant ministry as following God's command to be concerned with slums and God's children who cannot eat three square meals a day. King says preachers can talk about the "New Jerusalem," but what about the new New York, the new Atlanta, the new Memphis, and so on?

King then connects direct action with economic boycott. Though African Americans are poor when compared individually with white Americans, when taken all together the wealth of African Americans amounts to $30 billion a year, which is more than the national budget of Canada. King reminds African Americans of the power that they have, if they knew how to pool it. Because of this power, King believes that protesters do not have to curse, argue, or "go around acting bad with our words." For King, protesters do not need any brick, bottles, or Molotov cocktails. Protesters can simply withdraw their economic support and not buy Coca-Cola or Wonder Bread. King encourages investment in black banks and black insurance companies. He concludes this second movement by encouraging them to build an economic base and put pressure where it really hurts. This is what King believes to be a relevant ministry and announces that he is "always happy to see a relevant ministry."

Movement Three: "Thank God for allowing me to be here."

In the third movement, King begins to develop his preacher-voice, rhythm, and cadence. Embedded in the African American preaching tradition are code phrases that indicate the beginning of a climactic shift.

King uses such a code phrase when he says, "Now let me say as I move to my conclusion." In the African American preaching tradition, this particular code phrase functions in two ways: (1) to ask for the audience's patience in anticipation of some form of further extended argumentation, or (2) to signal that the speaker is about to ascend to the climactic utterance that will include inspiration and motivation primarily through the use of emotive material. While the phrase indicates some of the former, it functions much more to indicate the latter. King must build the rhetorical platform to help the audience ascend to celebration. When King says, "Now, let me say as I move to my conclusion that we've got to give ourselves in this struggle until the end," it is the announcement of the platform and the beginning of its construction with the concept of "dangerous unselfishness."

King uses typology and tells the biblical story of a man who came to Jesus looking for a philosophical debate about who was his neighbor (Luke 10:25–37). Jesus takes him down the Jericho road, and tells the story of a man who was mugged and left for dead. Two religious leaders pass the man by on their way to religious services, but the good Samaritan came by and helped the man. King relates that the priest and Levite that did not help the man because they asked, "If I stop to help this man, what will happen to me?" The good Samaritan came by and reversed the question and asked: "If I do not stop to help this man, what will happen to him?" King takes anaphoric fight and raises the emotional intensity. He calls protesters to "make America what it ought to be" and take the opportunity "to make America a better nation." He closes this third move with a connector from the first movement, "And I want to thank God, once more, for allowing me to be here with you." It almost sounds like a conclusion, but he shifts in the fourth movement, based on his emotion and intensity, to his sonorous preaching voice.

Movement Four: "I'm so happy that I didn't sneeze."

In the fourth movement of the speech, King moves fully into his preaching voice and the African American preaching tradition to confront and resolve the internal and external exigencies through celebration. He opens this movement with the story of being stabbed in New York City while signing books. He recounts that the blade was so close to his aorta that if he would have merely sneezed, he would have died. He got a letter from a little white girl in White Plains High School that said she was so "happy" that he did not sneeze. King again uses anaphora to raise the emotional intensity, "I too am happy that I did not sneeze. If I had sneezed, I would not have been around here in 1960 when students all over the south started sitting in at lunch counters." King repeats the panoramic view of history that we went on in the first part of the speech, only this time we are traversing the 1960s civil rights movement instead of all time. King offers six anaphoric "If I had sneezed" that precede, according to Miller, the seven great events of the civil rights movement—the Lunch Counter Sit-In, Freedom Rides, Albany campaign, Birmingham crusade, March on Washington, Selma-to-Montgomery March, and Memphis strike.[23] If he had sneezed, he would not have been around for these seven great events and with each "If I had sneezed," King raises the emotional intensity and pitch and the audience enthusiastically responds going higher and higher.

The audience is in full call and response mode now, not constraining the preacher in any way, but giving him permission to push to the depths of what is in his soul. King is being pushed to new heights of improvisational rhetorical brilliance. This was not the first time he had done the "If I had sneezed" set piece, but in this moment, in Memphis, King is resolving all internal and external exigencies, and he calls forth all the reserves of his moral imagination. The level of audience response is at least as great as, if not greater than, the last sections of either "I Have a Dream" or "Our God Is Marching On."

King gave the entire speech without notes or text. King had given thought to what he would say and had time on the way over to Mason Temple and during the introduction to collect his thoughts. What King could not plan was the call and response of the audience and audience participation as a prime influence in the shaping of the direction of the discourse. The audience's call and response pushed him and encouraged him to uncover and rhetorically symbolize what he deeply believes in his soul

---

23. Miller, 130.

(moral imagination). King concludes and resolves the fourth movement of the speech by repeating the line, "I'm so happy that I didn't sneeze."

Movement Five: "I'm happy tonight. I'm not worried about anything."

King now delivers the final and most spectacular movement of the speech. While the expectation is that he would now continue the upward movement in emotional celebrative intensity, he takes an emotive downturn. He says, "And they were telling me (pause). Now it doesn't matter now. It really doesn't matter what happens now." It is a radical pause, and his eyes widen a bit, as if he is collecting information from his soul, searching for connections that are deep in his soul, and I would say, deep in his moral imagination. The sentence is a gear shift, a downshift in the upward emotive intensity. It could be that he is taking his trademark downturn of the collision with reality in the midst of the upward celebration of the sermon. In the midst of several speeches, King in the closing upward celebrative movement brings the audience to stark reality. In the midst of the upward celebration in the close of "Our God Is Marching On," King's most optimistic and hopeful speech after the victory of marching from Selma to Montgomery, Alabama, he says:

> I must admit to you that there are some difficult days ahead. We are still in for a season of suffering in many of the black belt counties of Alabama, many areas of Mississippi, many areas of Louisiana. I must admit to you that there are still jail cells waiting for us, and dark and difficult moments.[24]

King sought to keep his discourse from being solely "pie-in-the-sky" religion that built false hope in a sweet afterlife and these downturns may include some of that. He makes this downturn of reality in the upward celebration of the close in Memphis because the call and response of the audience has freed him to face what is in his own soul—the reality of his own death, his resolution to his death, and its implications for the freedom struggle.

---

24. Martin Luther King Jr., "Our God Is Marching On," *The Martin Luther King, Jr. Research and Education Institute*, accessed April 2, 2017, https://kinginstitute.stanford.edu/our-god-marching.

For twelve years now he has lived with the constant concern about what would happen in regard to his death, but he begins to resolve the concern by recounting an example of such incidents that have kept him worried. He tells of the pilot coming on the public address system of that morning's flight to Memphis and apologizing for the delay. The pilot relates that Martin Luther King was on the plane and they had the plane guarded all night and the luggage was checked carefully to make sure that the flight was safe. He then mentions about coming into Memphis and some of the threats that were out about what would happen to him. We are at the heart of the speech now. We are at the bottom of his struggle with death in his own soul.

He continues, "Well, I don't know what will happen now. We've got some difficult days ahead." The downshift has been fully completed and the issue of his death is squarely on the table for all to see. "We [notice the *we*] have some difficult days ahead. But it really doesn't matter with me [personal pronoun] now because I [personal pronoun] have been to the mountaintop. And I [personal pronoun] do not mind." The mountaintop is a spiritual referent and the audience gets it instantly as a place of communication with God, such as Moses going up to the mountaintop and receiving the Ten Commandments. Because he has communicated with God, he is at peace with whatever happens. He mentions that like anybody he would like to live a long life and longevity has its place. He is not concerned with longevity; he just wants to do God's will. King concludes the speech in the height of emotive celebration:

> And he has allowed me to go up to the mountaintop and look over and I've seen the Promised Land. I may not get there with you, but we as a people will get to the Promised Land. And so I am not worried about anything. I'm not fearing any man. Mine eyes have seen the glory of the coming of the Lord.[25]

King is masterfully performing Moses to encourage himself and his audience. In Deuteronomy 34:1–5, Moses climbed Mount Nebo from the plains of Moab to the top of Pisgah. God showed him the promised

---

25. King, "I've Been to the Mountaintop."

land, but would not let him cross over into it. This was the final act of Moses's life, and then he died. King is performing this biblical narrative through the use of biblical typology. Just as King and God surveyed human history at the beginning of the speech, and just as King surveyed the civil rights movement of the 1950s and '60s, King and God now survey the end of his life and the victory of the civil rights movement. From this cosmic vantage point, King is announcing victory and resolving the exigencies with the fear of death and the assurance of cosmic victory, not only for himself, but for the movement and audience as well.

King is leaving the movement and the struggle in God's hand and to God's eschatological time. In "Beyond Vietnam," he concludes with human choice and the fact that humans must choose the kind of future that they want. But in this conclusion, very similar to "Our God Is Marching On," God is the prime mover. God took him up to the mountaintop. God showed him the promised land. God indicated that he would not enter it, and God assured him that the people would get there. God would win the victory. And because of what God has done and what God had showed him, he is able to say: "I'm happy, tonight." King's genius is to symbolize the victory rhetorically through the vehicle of the exodus-promised-land narrative, which is so centrally grounded in the hearts, lives, and experience of the primarily African American audience.

King attempts in the final sentence of the speech to quote, "The Battle Hymn of the Republic," but can only get one line out: "Mine eyes have seen the glory of the coming of the Lord!!" In *My Life with Martin Luther King, Jr.,* Coretta Scott King gives her interpretation of these final words of the speech:

> So intense was the audience's emotional response to Martin's words, so high was his own exaltation responding to their excitement, the action and reaction of one to the other, that he was overcome; he broke off there. I believe he intended to finish the quotation—"His truth is marching on." But he could not.[26]

---

26. Coretta Scott King, *My Life with Martin Luther King, Jr.* (New York: Holt, Rinehart and Winston, 1969), 316.

Other eyewitnesses and biographers agree with Coretta Scott King's interpretation. Or, in the terms of the African American church, "the Spirit" overwhelmed him. In either or both cases, it was God's cosmic victory manifest on earth in God's time. King gave himself to it, abandoned himself to it, and had no need to locate God's victory in human time. It was now faith in God and God alone, and he was overcome.

After not finishing the quotation, King turned, and with tears in his eyes fell into Ralph Abernathy's arms and his seat. While other ministers in the pulpit attended to him, pandemonium swept Mason Temple as the audience came to their feet, clapping, crying, and waving their hands. Many preachers were sobbing openly and there were many demonstrative shouts of joy and celebration. At the conclusion of his speeches, King would usually leave so as not to be swarmed by the crowd, but this night he stayed and shook hands with preachers and the people who made up such a compelling audience.

Many report that after the speech and the next day King was upbeat and buoyant. Many staffers and those close to King saw the speech as a resolution for King. Stephen Oates interprets the speech as resolution and quotes King's staffer Bernard Lee:

> One thing was certain; the speech and the warmth of the audience proved therapeutic for King. The anxiety that had bothered him before the address was gone now. "He had broken the cycle again," said [Bernard] Lee, "had broken the despair."[27]

Rev. Samuel "Billy" Kyles commented that "he preached the fear of death out of himself."[28] Not only did King offer resolution for himself, but he also offered resolution for many in the audience. Rev. James Smith, said: "There was an overcoming mood, an overcoming spirit in that place. When Dr. King spoke that night we knew that we were going to win."[29] Lewis A. Sussman believes the speech was a resolution as well:

---

27. Stephen B. Oates, *Let the Trumpet Sound: The Life of Martin Luther King, Jr.* (New York: New American Library, 1982), 486.

28. Rev. Samuel "Billy" Kyles, personal interview by the author.

29. Michael K. Honey, *Going Down Jericho Road: The Memphis Strike and Martin Luther King's Last Campaign* (New York: W. W. Norton, 2007), 424–25.

Contemporary sources relate that there was, indeed, something different about King's speech that night. For he had already faced and discussed many times the countless threats, attempted assassination, physical assaults, violent heckling, and bomb attacks during his career. Yet that night King seemed not only to recognize the danger of violent death, but even more so, energized by the responsiveness and the enthusiasm of the audience, to have reached a spiritual ease and peace with that likelihood.[30]

In "I've Been to the Mountaintop," King articulates the cosmic resolution of God buried deep in his belief system and moral imagination. I want to turn now to discuss the qualities of moral imagination that are located in "I've Been to the Mountaintop."

Four Qualities of the Moral Imagination

The four qualities of the moral imagination are:

1. Equality envisioned and represented by physical presence

2. Death as a catalyst or bridge to create opportunities to overcome the past and make new decisions for peace and justice

3. Wisdom in ancient texts and sources of truth

4. Address the audience in the language of poetry and art that lifts and elevates the human spirit by touching the emotive chords of wonder, mystery, and hope.

I want to apply these qualities to King's words in his speech/sermon "I've Been to the Mountaintop."

In regard to equality envisioned and represented by physical presence, the most obvious fact is that the "I've Been to the Mountaintop" speech/sermon was only possible because King brought his concern and physical

---

30. Lewis A. Sussman, "The Classical References in Martin Luther King's Last Speech and the Meaning of 'I've Been to the Mountaintop,'" *Classical Bulletin* 81, no. 1 (2005): 65.

presence to Memphis to help sanitation workers. This was an act of solidarity in a long list of acts of solidarity for movements of freedom and equality starting in 1954 with the Montgomery bus boycott. King put his concern and physical presence on the line in numerous ways every day of the civil rights movement as he was jailed; stabbed; assaulted with rocks and bricks; battered psychologically with jeers, hate-filled names and messages, death threats, pressure, harassment, and manipulations; this even from his own government. King was ultimately shot and killed because of his work for peace and justice, because of his concern for the vulnerable, and in this instance, the sanitation workers in Memphis.

The second category of moral imagination is death as a catalyst or bridge to create opportunities to overcome the past and make new decisions for peace and justice. Edwin C. Appel, in his article, "The Rhetoric of Dr. Martin Luther King, Jr.: Comedy and Context in Tragic Collision," following Kenneth Burke, notes the change in the content and style of King's speeches/sermons toward the end of his life (1967–68). The belief in the cultural myth of America of early King, he calls a "comic" frame. The later King of moral culpability and structural flaws, he calls a "tragic" frame. He argues that from the tragic frame, King made the painful choice to die symbolically himself rather than visit "symbolic destruction" upon his opponents as the tragic frame requires. Appel writes:

> A tragic actor in a tragic scene with tragic enemies and tragic goals in place cannot easily elude tragic action of some cast or kind. King did not. Ineluctably, the curve of his rhetoric followed the curve of his career, directly toward a sacrificial death that, in his case, atoned for the public disorder his rhetoric energized. As a sacrificial "vessel," King was eminently "worthy": "legalistically" to segregationists, "fatalistically" to many detached observers, and profoundly innocently to his followers and friends.[31]

Appel maintains that his death helped to heal a nation torn apart by racial strife. The picture of George Wallace and black citizens of Alabama embracing in reconciled friendship, symbolically for Appel, captured the myriad of ways that King's sacrifice helped heal a nation. For many, this is

---

31. Edwin C. Appel, "The Rhetoric of Dr. Martin Luther King, Jr.: Comedy and Context in Tragic Collision," *Western Journal of Communication* 61 no. 4 (Fall 1997): 399.

the common understanding of King's life and death, he sacrificially gave his life to help heal America.

The third quality of moral imagination is wisdom found in ancient texts and sources of truth. For King, the Bible was the chief source of wisdom and truth, particularly the Hebrew prophets and Jesus. Lischer suggests that following the Selma march of 1965 (the first era of King's moral imagination), King appealed less to the Constitution and Declaration of Independence and leaned more heavily on the Bible.[32] This would be consistent with King's sense that equality and freedom would occur primarily because of God and become less dependent on human choice and action. On numerous occasions of the movement and marches, over and over again in his speeches and sermons, and even in this final speech/sermon, with the parable of the good Samaritan from Luke as an example, King consults the Bible as the source of wisdom and truth for wise and just living. In Memphis, and in every civil rights struggle, King appropriated the Bible in support of the local struggle for equality, and in this instance, for garbage workers in Memphis.

Along with the Bible, King received a broad and expansive Western liberal arts education in prestigious American schools exposing him to many sources of wisdom and truth, including European philosophers, distinguished American preachers and theologians, and the tremendous influence of Gandhi. King gained wisdom from the mentorship, sermons, and teachings of generations of black people and intellectual preachers, including his father and grandfather.

The fourth quality of moral imagination is that of addressing the audience in the language of poetry and art that lifts and elevates the human spirit by touching the emotive chords of wonder, mystery, and hope. This too is obvious, given the rhetorical power of King's oratory. "I've Been to the Mountaintop" is only one of the many fine examples of rhetorical and theological genius and the power of King's oratory to evoke wonder, mystery, and hope. Richard Lischer called King the most influential orator

---

32.   Lischer, 17.

of the twentieth century that sought to "redeem the moral and political character of a nation." [33]

There is a place in my soul, as an African American person, that still grieves and laments the assassination of Martin Luther King Jr. I have stood on the very spot, the balcony of the Lorraine Motel in Memphis, where King was shot and killed, and discovered that there are some griefs and losses that you learn to live with, but the pain is ever-present. For the apostle of nonviolence, the one who gave his concern and physical presence to the needs of others, to the very point of his life, to witness the selfish disregard for the vulnerable and the restraining of freedom and equality to oneself and one's group brings me more pain than I care to deal with at times. I wrote this chapter as a requiem, as a way to mourn, keep alive, grieve, and make possible freedom and equality in the present moment by understanding the moral imagination of Martin Luther King Jr., even if freedom and equality has to be at God's hand and in God's time.

Requiem

I placed Requiem in the title of this chapter because it seems that too often those who have the moral imagination to see freedom and equality for the entire human family, and actually embody it, and take concrete steps to make it a reality, are often persecuted and killed. This was certainly the case for Robert F. Kennedy, Martin Luther King Jr., and many others who could be named. A Requiem or Requiem Mass, also known as Mass for the Dead, is a mass in the Catholic Church offered for the repose of the soul or souls of one or more deceased persons, using a particular form of the Roman Missal. According to the dictionary, "Requiem" is the accusative singular form of the Latin noun *requies,* "rest, repose." [34] Requiem also came to be defined as any sacred composition that sets to music religious texts that would be appropriate at a funeral, and has subsequently been

---

33. Richard Lischer, *The Preacher King: Martin Luther King, Jr. and the Word That Moved America* (New York: Oxford University Press, 1995), bookcover.

34. *Merriam-Webster Online,* s.v. "Requiem," accessed August 31, 2017, https://www.merriam -webster.com/dictionary/requiem.

applied to other musical compositions associated with death, dying, and mourning, even when they lack religious or liturgical relevance.

Webber composed *Requiem,* a Requiem Mass, after learning about the story of a Cambodian boy who was forced to murder his mutilated sister or be executed himself, and the death of a journalist who had interviewed Webber and was killed in IRA conflicts in Ireland. Both tragedies struck nerves deep to his core and Webber wrote music as a way to cope with his grief and loss. When he finished *Requiem,* he dedicated it to his father who passed away in 1982. Sarah Brightman, in her performance of the "Pie Jesu," the most well-known part of the *Requiem,* says Webber dedicated it to close friends and family members who are no longer with us. In the "Pie Jesu," Webber combined the text of the traditional Pie Jesu with that of the version of the Agnus Dei.

I want to close this chapter that is written to encourage preachers everywhere to preach moral imagination such that we might not have so much loss and grief by paraphrasing the words of Webber's "Pie Jesu."

Agnus Dei,	Lamb of God,
Qui tollis peccata mundi,	Who takes away the sins of the world,
Dona eis requiem,	Give them rest,
Sempiternam	Everlasting
Requiem.	Rest.

May the God, who takes away the sin of the world, grant to King and Kennedy, and all who are persecuted and die in the struggle for freedom and equality everywhere, everlasting rest.

WHO IS THE MORAL LEADER OF OUR NATION?

FOUR QUALITIES OF MORAL IMAGINATION AND THE NEW MORAL LEADERSHIP

Trust is a transaction between the leaders and those they lead. Throughout our history, the deeply held beliefs of various Presidents have taken the nation into war, delayed the pursuit of peace, alienated enemies, appeased enemies. At other times, presidential beliefs have conquered the continent, freed the slaves, taken us to the moon because a president firmly believed we could get there. As citizens, it is vital that we be able to believe our President; it is also vital that we know what he believes, and why. This President has made both a severe challenge.

Nancy Gibbs

I n this chapter, I will explore how the four qualities of the moral imagination can offer critique and challenge to any leadership, and in this case, the leadership of our nation. Discerning the four qualities of the moral imagination allows estimation of leadership above and beyond the normal identity politics, divisions, and categories of race, class, religion, gender, political labels, or parties, and so on. Critique, challenge, and when appropriate, celebration are part of preaching dangerous sermons, and so I raise the questions of the moral imagination here in order to model and motivate other preachers to join in the task of preaching dangerous sermons.

Far too often, morals and ethics are established based upon the norms of our group. This usually means that if our group does it, it must be moral, and if another group does it, it must be obviously and utterly immoral and wrong. This situational ethic is established from a pessimistic, divisive, and combative zero-sum game imagination and worldview. In this mindset, our group must win at all costs, and anyone not of our group must be the loser and enemy, even at the cost of truth, logic, and common sense. This situational ethic is based in the idolatrous and diabolical imagination.

From the perspective of the four qualities of the moral imagination, right is right and wrong is wrong, regardless of the group, political party, or any human classifications or categories of person. This is consistent with the wisdom of the ages: Truth is broader, wider, higher, and deeper than our narrow delineations of the limited situational and zero-sum game ethics of our group. Therefore, the truth of these four qualities of moral imagination can be applied to leadership in order to discern whether or not it is moral. Leadership, including that of the preacher, has an inordinate amount of influence upon the moral imagination of a group. Russell Kirk says, "We become what others, in a voice of authority, tell us we are or ought to be."[1] I want to start by asking this question: Who is the moral leader of our nation?

The Moral Leader of Our Nation

On March 25, 1968, ten days before he was killed, Martin Luther King Jr. was invited to respond to questions before the Sixty-Eighth

1. Fennell, "What Is Moral Imagination?"

Annual Convention of the Rabbinical Assembly. He was introduced that evening by Rabbi Abraham Joshua Heschel and in the introduction of King, Heschel asked, "Where does moral religious leadership come from in America today?" Heschel continued:

> Where does God dwell in America today? . . . Is He at home with those who are complacent, indifferent to other people's agony, devoid of mercy? Is He not rather with the poor and the contrite in the slums? Dark is the world for me, for all its cities and stars. If not for the few signs of God's radiance who could stand such agony, such darkness? Where do we hear a voice like the prophets of Israel? . . . Martin Luther King is a voice, a vision and a way. I call upon every Jew to harken to his voice, to share his vision, to follow in his way.[2]

Rabbi Heschel labeled King as the moral leader of America. Of whom could this statement be made in America? Who is the moral leader of our nation? Who is it that we could consider a voice, a vision for us all? To whose moral voice would we harken and follow in their way? To whose voice would we have our children share in their vision and ethics?

Some would argue that the time of single and solitary moral leadership is over; moral leadership is more diffused and local in its expression than one national charismatic moral leader. This is true that we have moral expectations of our priests, rabbis, imams, ministers, teachers, coaches, principles, parents, neighbors, and so on of moral leadership that is indigenous and disseminated. Yet, we also have the expectation of moral leadership from our national religious leaders and elected officials, especially the symbol, office, and power of the presidency of the United States. According to the four qualities of moral imagination that we have outlined herein, at the time of this writing we have an enormous absence of moral leadership in Donald J. Trump, and therefore we are in moral crisis and moral emergency. Based in our idolatrous and diabolical imagination, there is a loose adherence to these four qualities of the moral imagination in our culture. We lack sufficient moral leadership at the local and national level,

---

2. Martin Luther King Jr., interview with Professor Abraham Joshua Heschel at the Sixty-Eigth Annual Convention of the Rabbinical Assembly, March 25, 1968, "Conversation with Martin Luther King, Jr.," http://gendlergrapevine.org/wp-content/uploads/2013/06/Conversation-with-Martin-Luther-King .pdf.

in churches, public institutions, CEOs, business leaders, politicians, and so on, all who disproportionately set the moral tone of our nation. While there are many people exhibiting high-quality moral leadership at all of these levels, the general context in which this leadership is executed is the idolatrous and diabolical imagination.

I will take each of the four qualities of moral imagination and offer commentary as the substance to the argument as to why we are in a moral emergency. As a reminder, let me again list the four qualities of moral imagination: (1) envision equality and represent it by one's physical presence; (2) empathy as a catalyst or bridge to create opportunities to overcome the past and make new decisions for peace and justice; (3) wisdom and truth in ancient texts, the wisdom of the ages; and (4) the language of poetry and art that lifts and elevates by touching the emotive chords of wonder, hope, and mystery.

Envision equality and represent that by one's physical presence

At its base, consistent with the first moral quality, moral imagination involves an inclusive vision of freedom and equality for all, and not just in words, but also in deeds, such as to put one's physical presence, or even reputation, on the line. Caught within the grips of white supremacy, indicative of the idolatrous and diabolical imagination, we often lack moral courage, and are not up to the task of envisioning equality and freedom for all. We offer lip service to equality, but when it comes to deeds and actions that involve our physical presence and risk, many of us shy away, and are often innocent, naïve, or blind to realities of injustice and inequality. Within our present idolatrous and diabolical imagination, there is even the need to defend the progress for equality that was made during the civil rights movement. Recently, hate groups that were dismissed to the shadows and the fringe of American discourse after the civil rights movement, have retrenched, and now they openly and directly operate and state their support of white supremacy and opposition to equality.

Richard Hofstadter, in his classic work, *The Paranoid Style in American Politics*, has defined a destructive disposition in American politics that is presently operative at the highest levels of power and authority in America. He called it "the paranoid style of American politics." Hofstadter gives a clear explanation:

> I believe there is a style of mind that is far from new and that is not necessarily right-wing. I call it the paranoid style simply because no other word adequately evokes the sense of heated exaggeration, suspiciousness, and conspiratorial fantasy that I have in mind. In using the expression "paranoid style" I am not speaking in a clinical sense, but borrowing a clinical term for other purposes.... In fact, the idea of the paranoid style as a force in politics would have little contemporary relevance or historical value if it were applied only to men (and women) with profoundly disturbed minds. It is the use of paranoid modes of expression by more or less normal people that makes the phenomenon significant.[3]

Hofstadter suggests that American politics has often been an arena for angry minds. Angry minds, animosities, and passions of a small minority can wield a tremendous amount of political leverage.

Giving further clarity to the mind of the paranoid style, Hofstadter says those of the paranoid mind feel dispossessed:

> America has been largely taken away from them and their kind, though they are determined to try to repossess it and to prevent the final destructive act of subversion. The old American virtues have already been eaten away by cosmopolitans and intellectuals; the old competitive capitalism has been gradually undermined by socialistic and communistic schemers; the old national security and independence have been destroyed by treasonous plots, having as their most powerful agents not merely outsiders and foreigners as of old but major statesmen who are at the very centers of American power. Their predecessors had discovered foreign conspiracies; the modern radical right finds that conspiracy also embraces conspiracies at home.[4]

The paranoid style is pervasive at the top levels of government. For example, Donald Trump tweets out false accusations, statements, and lies on a regular basis. As an example, one tweet against former President Obama

---

3. Richard Hofstadter, *The Paranoid Style in American Politics and Other Essays* (Cambridge: Harvard University Press, 1996), 3–4.

4. Ibid., 23.

was based upon conspiracy theories sourced from information based in the paranoid style.[5] Any information based in the paranoid style (conspiracy theories, non-fact-based sources, accusations, and unsubstantiated claims) cannot be moral leadership. Nancy Gibbs reports that voters were not deceived: "Nearly two-thirds said that Trump was not trustworthy, including nearly a third of people who voted for him anyway." Gibbs concludes: "Dishonesty in a candidate, far from being disqualifying, became a badge of 'disruption.' "[6]

It is important to realize that this paranoid style is not only pervasive at the highest levels of government, but also in the church, family, home, businesses, and so on of many normal and average people. Its "normal-ness" is how leaders of the paranoid style get elected in the first place. In part, I write this book to oppose the paranoid style becoming normalized. Blatant and repetitive dishonesty is a lack of moral character and a disqualification for leadership, and especially the highest office in the land. This paranoid style was once at the fringe of American life, but now has legitimized itself, and is now granted access and a voice at the center of our government. The paranoid style, whenever and wherever it occurs, is the opposite of inclusion and freedom for all, and as a result, though it is natural to human nature, it is not moral. It is evidence of a lack of moral imagination. The paranoid style is based in the idolatrous and diabolical imagination.

Empathy as a catalyst or bridge to create new opportunities for peace and justice

While we celebrate that America has released more creative imagination and energy into the world than any modern nation in history,

---

5. On March 4, 2017, at 6:30 a.m., President Trump tweeted "Terrible! Just found out that Obama had my 'wires tapped' in Trump Tower just before the victory. Nothing found. This is McCarthyism!" At 6:49 a.m., he tweeted, "Is it legal for a sitting President to be "wire tapping" a race for president prior to an election? Turned down by court earlier. A NEW LOW!" To date, Donald Trump has provided no factual basis for the allegations and most sources conclude the information was not gained from government sources. Donald Trump became aware of a recent *Breitbart* article based on a Mark Levin radio segment quoted on Fox News. For the clearest discussion of this and the falsehoods and lies of Donald Trump see Michael Scherer, "Can President Trump Handle the Truth?" *Time Magazine,* March 23, 2017, http://time.com/4710614/donald-trump-fbi-surveillance-house-intelligence-committee/.

6. Nancy Gibbs, "When a President Can't Be Taken at His Word," *Time Magazine,* March 23, 2017, http://time.com/4710615/donald-trump-truth-falsehoods/.

America has also been imperialistic and violent on an unparalleled level. The question of this second characteristic of moral equality that must be asked is how empathy can help us to make new choices to overcome the past and contemporary violence and oppression. I want to suggest that within the idolatrous and diabolical imagination we have lost much of the sense of empathy in this nation, and whenever empathy is lost, therefore we are not moral. The result is that we only have empathy for people of our group or tribe.

In one of my earlier books, *American Dream 2.0: A Christian Way Out of the Great Recession*, I ask this question: What is the centrality that holds this nation together?[7] What is the common vision that unifies us? What is the common mission of America that we all share such to the extent that we would be willing to sacrifice personal interest to see the vision become a reality? What is the dream of America? The American Dream is a socially-constructed concept and identity based upon the adoption and agreement on certain values and principles. What values and principles do we share such that we might call our agreement, the common good? What would we be willing to sacrifice for the common good? Empathy is the value upon which we shape principles that we call the common good. Without empathy, what we have is special-interest groups in-fighting to become winners and losers in the downward spiral and destructive zero-sum game of the idolatrous and diabolical imagination.

A nation based in the idolatrous and diabolical imagination becomes a nation of special interests, and each special interest is more concerned about their special interest than the interest of the whole, or the common good. In such a nation, each self-preserving special interest has one common mantra: "Don't touch my..." Don't touch my guns, welfare, mortgage interest deductions, military and prison industrial complex, Medicare and Social Security, defense spending, farm subsidies, tax breaks, corporate welfare, and so on. When we get through with the political shenanigans, distractions, smokescreens, back-room deals, blaming, fearmongering, insults, and pettiness that operates as much political discussion in our nation, what we mean and our bottom line is do not touch my benefits and interests, and my privilege, especially my white privledge.

---

7. Thomas, *American Dream 2.0: A Christian Way Out of the Great Recession.*

Because of the loss of empathy and the focus on special interests, we have lost the concept of sacrifice, in and for the nation. When was the last time any of our political leadership called this nation to sacrifice? Would it be for the war effort in World War II that the nation was called to sacrifice? It is almost like in contemporary culture sacrifice for the nation is taboo, a bad word, except for soldiers, military families, and a very few others. Have we lost the ability to sacrifice for the common good? We cannot sacrifice if there is not enough empathy to support a common vision. Without empathy, America is about my group and our rights and what we can get, what we can protect, and as result, "Do not touch my." We live in the America of our benefit, and as long as we exclusively focus on our benefit, or the benefit of our group alone, we cannot develop levels of empathy for unity and a common vision. Many people have given their lives for freedom. When was the last time that we have been asked to give up anything? When was the last time our nation was asked to sacrifice, or give up anything, for the common good?

I long for the time in America that President John F. Kennedy made the moral statement: "Ask not what your country can do for you, but what you can do for your country." After the attacks of 9/11, we were not asked to sacrifice anything. We were asked to go shopping to sustain the economy. We are not able to call the nation to sacrifice because there is not enough empathy to generate a vision of unity and the common good. Our determined self-interest to the exclusion of empathy is not moral. As we will see when we briefly discuss David Hume in this chapter, empathy is a catalyst of the moral imagination and the decline of empathy is connected to our participation in the idolatrous and diabolical imagination. In 2017 we have a president who only has empathy for his "base" and not all of the American people.

Wisdom and truth in ancient texts: The wisdom of the ages

Overall, the role of truth in the idolatrous and diabolical imagination is ambiguous, self-serving, based in public relations, manipulative, destructive, fearmongering, and in its worst manifestation, even death-dealing. One of the tricks and manipulations in both the idolatrous and diabolical imagination is to divorce truth from its ancient roots, that is, to disconnect, disrupt, or sever people's experience and thought from the wisdom of the ages; the universal library of human knowledge and the transcendental wisdom that guides humankind; and to create divergent, alternative reality. I want to be specific about truth in both the idolatrous imagination and diabolical imagination in order to clearly illustrate what is done to truth, and then, talk about the process of how truth becomes a lie and a lie becomes the truth. The bottom line is truth in the idolatrous and diabolical imagination diverges from the wisdom of the ages, and creates an alternative falsehood that is peddled as reality.

As an example of the idolatrous imagination, truth becomes, in Donald Trump's words, "truthful hyperbole." Truthful hyperbole is an innocent form of exaggeration that is used mostly in terms of promotion and profile-raising. Trump claims in *Trump: The Art of the Deal* "that people want to believe that something is the biggest and the greatest and the most spectacular."[8] Our earlier definition of idolatrous imagination is the honoring of the celebrity culture of sports, music, movies, and television based upon the prepackaging, advertising, and mass marketing of mainstream corporate media. It is the creation of the truthful hyperbole, the spectacular, stunning, dazzling, and the over-the-top because people want to believe in the biggest and the greatest.

In idolatrous imagination, we regularly create and invent the spectacular. Daniel Boorstin coins the phrase "pseudo-events" and argues that we create spectacular pseudo-events with the intent to deceive.[9] Boorstin quotes Edward L. Bernays, of whom we shall say much more later, in his pioneering work, *Crystallizing Public Opinion*. Bernays suggests that the owners of a hotel want to increase the hotel's prestige, and therefore business. Of course, they could do it the old-fashioned way, hire a new chef, paint the rooms, improve service, and so on. But instead, they decide to consult a public relations firm and the firm recommends staging a celebration of the hotel's thirtieth anniversary. They are instructed to form

---

8. Jacob Steinberg, "Who Controls the Past Controls the Future," *The Wake*, March 13, 2017, http://www.wakemag.org/sections/voices/controls-past-controls-future.

9. Boorstin, *The Image: A Guide to Psuedo-Events in America* (New York: Vintage, 1992).

a high-profile anniversary committee, including a prominent banker, a leading society matron, a well-known lawyer, and an influential preacher. An "event" is planned, a banquet to call attention to the distinguished service the hotel has given the community.

The celebration is held, photographs are taken, the occasion is widely reported, and the object is accomplished. Once the celebration has been held, the celebration itself becomes evidence that the hotel really is a distinguished institution. The occasion actually gives the hotel the prestige to which it is pretending. They have not changed one thing: they did not paint a wall, hire a chef, or improve service, but with public relations they threw a pseudo-event. In the idolatrous imagination in America, we make pseudo-events. With our television and marketing, we have created the spectacular, announced that we are great and grand, but we have not changed the basics, such as our character, our inclusion, or our equality for all.

Truth in the diabolical imagination delights in the subhuman and perverse. It is the theory and justification of the subjection and oppression of people by making others subhuman through theological, political, economic, or even scientific validations. It is the doctrinal validation and substantiation of imperialism, violence, empire, and conquest of indigenous people. Its tools are hate, fear, discrimination, racism, slavery, misogyny, homophobia, genocide, xenophobia, cynicism, anti-immigrant discourse, and so on. It is cultural myth perpetrated by psychological warfare to suggest that one group deserves superiority based upon self-serving criteria. It is the justifications that are given for white supremacy such as a city set up on a hill, manifest destiny, the American Dream, and American exceptionalism, which always concludes with the overwhelming majority of goods, services, and resources in the hands of Euro-Americans and their descendants.

Russell Kirk argues that the diabolic imagination dominates most popular fiction, television, and theaters, including pornography, because it panders to the lust for violence, destruction, cruelty, and sensational disorder—the spectacular. Much of this content is standard fare on prime time television, Hollywood scripts, cable networks, advertising and marketing of the commercial airwaves that result in a lack of moral imagination, often with the direct intent to sell products regardless of deception. It might be that what separates the idolatrous and diabolical imagination is the measure on a spectrum of the intent to deceive. The diabolical imagination is singularly lacking in moral imagination. As an example of the treatment of truth by the idolatrous and diabolical imagination, let me turn quickly to how truth becomes a lie and a lie becomes the truth.

There is a chapter titled "The Re-Channeling of History" in Edward Hooper's classic pioneering work, *The River: A Journey to the Source of HIV and AIDS*; in it, Hooper points out that pathological liars are rare.[10] Most people are honest if only because that is the easiest way to live with the most self-respect and a minimum of complications. However, for most people there does seem to be a sliding scale, a point at which lying becomes an option. Many will lie when their self-image is threatened, or their financial future is at stake, or when they need to protect their family or friends. Only a few people have the integrity to tell the truth regardless of the circumstances or the consequences. Most of us have integrity on some form of sliding scale.

Hooper goes on to say that the process of lying is interesting. One starts by swerving around the sharper and more dangerous corners of what is known to be true to arrive at a position that is almost true. This allows one to maintain two parallel versions of the truth: one for the heart, or perhaps the best friend, or for the spouse in the dead of night, and the other, less precise version for the potential enemy, for the person who asks awkward questions, and for those who might do one harm. Time passes. Recollections become less sharp. The two parallel versions of truth fade in and out and intertwine. Finally, the process is completed. Two apples become three apples, a chimp changes to a giraffe, a zebra to a crocodile, and the truth becomes a lie. Remembering becomes an issue, and as far as one remembers, one was not even there at the time in question. It is by this process that we re-channel history.

---

10. Edward Hooper, *The River: A Journey to the Source of HIV and AIDS* (Boston: Back Bay Books, 2000), 795.

Hooper makes the point that human nature has two sets of truth, one for the friend and the other for the enemy or potential enemy, and the real truth can get mixed up. Given the reality of our large and complex communication systems (i.e., Twitter, Facebook, Snapchat, cable networks, and so on), and the now exposed Russian interference through the utilization of social media platforms, the major contemporary question and dilemma in America is: What is the truth?

Time Magazine compared this question to the question it asked on its iconic cover in April 1966, "Is God Dead?" based upon several theologians debating the question of God's death in response to the national and global tragic happenings "as a summons to reflect on the meaning of existence." Based upon the fact that 97 percent of pollsters told Americans that they believe in God, the issue sparked lively debate. With the March 23, 2017, cover reading "Is Truth Dead?," echoing the 1966 cover, Nancy Gibbs says:

> Half a century later, I suspect that about as many people say they believe in Truth, and yet we find ourselves having an intense debate over its role and power in the face of a President who treats it like a toy. The old adage that "a lie gets halfway around the world before Truth has a chance to get its pants on" was true even before the invention of Twitter. But is has been given new relevance by an early rising Chief Executive and his smartphone.[11]

Based upon the large divisions and splintering into interest groups and factions, there is so much re-channeling of history that it gets difficult for the truth to be known. Spin was once the term in common parlance for re-channeling of history, but more recently, we have moved beyond spin and adopted "fake news," "alternative facts," and "alternative information." Systems of relentless fact-checking have emerged, and they are critically important, but there is also the human reality of a "confirmation bias" that Emma Roller comments on in her op-ed, "Your Facts or Mine":

> The strongest bias in American politics is not a liberal bias or a conservative bias; it is a confirmation bias, or the urge to believe only things that confirm what you already believe to be true. Not only do we tend to seek out and

---

11. Gibbs, "When a President Can't Be Taken at His Word."

remember information that reaffirms what we already believe, but there is also a "backfire effect," which sees people doubling down on their beliefs after being presented with evidence that contradicts them.[12]

My concern is, given our reality of idolatrous and diabolical imagination, that for some, the intent is to deceive and demean for self-serving purposes. Operating out of the paranoid, divisive, and combative zero-sum game imagination and worldview, people are divided into supporters and antagonists, and anyone not of our supportive group has to be the enemy. Truth and the very fabric of our moral imagination are threatened by these paranoid practices of our idolatrous and diabolical imagination.

Philip Davis from the financial investment community sums up my position from the perspective of the third quality of the moral imagination, the wisdom of the ages:

> You know we have reached peak ignorance when CNBC's Joe Kernein this morning said: "Well you know his 'fake' news is my real news and I bet my real news is his fake news, so it's all just a matter of perspective." No Joe, it isn't. There are such things as objective facts.[13]

Beyond the idolatrous and diabolical imagination consisting of spin, fake news, and alternative facts, there is an objective reality; and it is dangerous when the leader of our nation plays fast and loose with the facts. A presidency based in the idolatrous and diabolical imagination that re-channels truth is dangerous. I believe there are objective facts, truth, and principles that have been time-tested and reside in the collective unconscious. We have learned that some behaviors, such as lying and falsehood, bring discord and violence, and that truth and love bring peace and justice. The endgame of lies and falsehood is death and the endgame of truth is life. Though we have evolved ourselves into a nation of the idolatrous and diabolical imagination, there are people of all races, gender, political parties, and so on who are people of moral imagination, people of truth. I have

12. Emma Roller, "Your Facts or Mine," *New York Times,* October 25, 2016, https://www.nytimes.com/2016/10/25/opinion/campaign-stops/your-facts-or-mine.html.

13. Phillip Davis, "Merry Monday Market Madness Continues," *Seeking Alpha,* December 19, 2016, http://seekingalpha.com/article/4031394-merry-monday-market-madness-continues.

hope in the moral imagination of these harbingers of truth. This brings us perfectly to the fourth quality of the moral imagination, the language of poetry and art that lifts and elevates by touching the emotive chords of wonder, hope, and mystery.

The language of poetry and art that lifts and elevates

If our culture is primarily operating in the idolatrous and diabolical imagination, then what is the language that lifts and elevates by touching the chords of wonder, hope, and mystery? Let's look closely at the language of these imaginations and see if they elevate by touching the chords of wonder, hope, and mystery. First, the language of the idolatrous imagination is that of celebrity culture (i.e., marketing, public relations, branding, self-promotion, and advertising). The creation of the spectacular can be the false language of wonder and mystery that leads to exaggeration, over-stylized entertainment as escapism, and distraction from the inescapable realities of life. Most readers would be familiar with Neil Postman's book, *Amusing Ourselves to Death: Public Discourse in the Age of Show Business,* where he argues rational argument is diminished in the medium of television.[14] Politics, religions, information, and "breaking news," are commodities that are pre-packaged and sold for their entertainment value. Therefore, television news-as-entertainment is an example of discourse in the age of show business; it cannot be taken seriously, but often, and in most cases, it is. Idolatrous imagination and celebrity culture do not lift and elevate by touching the chords of wonder, hope, and mystery. They create a false diversion of entertainment as escapism as a source and fountain of truth.

Secondly, in the diabolical imagination, the language is often dystopian. *Webster's* defines dystopia as "an imaginary place where people are unhappy and usually afraid because they are not treated fairly."[15] Dystopia is the imagined and exaggerated state that everything in culture and

14. Neil Postman, *Amusing Ourselves to Death: Public Discourse in the Age of Show Business* (New York: Penguin Group, 1985).

15. *Merriam-Webster Online,* s.v. "dystopia," accessed August 29, 2017, https://www.merriam-webster.com/dictionary/dystopia.

society is unpleasant and bad. The made-up state of the community or society is such that people are living frightening, undesirable, and dehumanized lives. The diabolical imagination is distinctly and often dystopian.

Usually, the next step in dystopian rhetoric is to identify source(s) of dystopia that result in scapegoating, blaming, and the establishment an enemy to disparage, often minorities and immigrants. The complete opposite of governing out of the moral imagination is to govern out of dystopia. Many have commented on the dystopian tenor of Donald Trump's presidential campaign, his inauguration speech, and his administration, summed up in his "press is the enemy of the people" governing style. At some point, America will have to account for the cultural idolatrous and diabolical imagination that makes possible and necessary such candidates to govern.

How did we get to the point where dystopian rhetoric would hold such sway and power in our culture and election? This is a very complex question, and certainly out of the purview of this book for a comprehensive explanation, but let me offer a few thoughts that might fit into a larger explanation. Let me expand further on my discussion in the last section on spectacular events, spin, fake news, and alternative facts.

The beginnings of our descent into the idolatrous and diabolical imagination could be traced to the early period of the twentieth century, when because of the large-scale and complex nature of American society, according to author Stewart Ewen, two major beliefs became fashionable and operative: (1) services were required of a core of experts who specialized in the analysis and management of public opinion, and (2) the public was fundamentally illogical and techniques of communication must be identified and mastered to have effect on public opinion, attitudes, and thinking.[16] In the beginning and middle decades of the twentieth century, two men rose as the cardinal creators and advocates of public opinion management, and so much so, that their thinking and practice dominates even now in the first decades of the twenty-first century, Walter Lippmann and Edward L. Bernays. Lippman primarily did the intellectual framing

---

16. Stuart Ewen, "Unseen Engineers: Biography of an Idea," *PR!: A Social History of Spin* (New York: Basic Books, 1996), 146–73.

and Bernays applied many of the theories of Lippmann to general practice in order to actually influence public opinion. Lippmann developed the concept of "manufactured consent" to signify the constructed support of the masses for executive action as the resolution of the dialectical tension of citizen participation and the need for executive leaders to act.

Lippman assumed that as the world got larger and larger, it became increasingly more difficult for people to make sense of their world based upon their immediate experience. Because human behavior was little inclined to logic and public opinion was essentially an irrational force, mass-mediated words and pictures could present a "credible—though fallacious—pseudo-environment" to order thought and behavior.[17] Human reflexes are conditioned, that is, the way people see and experience their world is established by their cultural milieu, commonly held ways of seeing and experiencing reality, or "the habits of our eyes." We do not see first and then define, we define first and then we see. Because the world is so large and confusing, we basically perceive what our culture has defined and stereotyped for us. According to Lippman:

> Highly charged with the feelings that are attached to them, a given culture's repertoire of stereotypes is the glue that binds people to one another in a group, providing them with the underpinnings of their 'universe,' establishing the invisible "fortress" by which they maintain their tradition(s).[18]

My mind went immediately to white supremacy as a "habit of the eyes" and the invisible fortress of America. All of us are given a set of stereotypes through which to see the world. It is only through intense and careful scrutiny and observation that we can see those stereotypes and make up our minds about what we believe and what we subsequently act upon. This is the process of becoming "conscious" and the full maturing of the human mind. Initially, culture and parents give us beliefs, and with maturity, we evaluate and decide what we believe, what of our culture and parents to keep, and what to discard.

---

17. Ibid., 148.

18. Walter Lippman, *Public Opinion* (New York: Harcourt, Brace, and Co., 1922), 89, 95–96.

Because human reflexes are conditioned, Lippmann utilized the tools of social and psychological sciences to uncover the "habits of people's eyes." It is at this point, the decision to use psychological sciences to uncover the "habits of eyes," that begins the descent into the idolatrous and diabolical imagination: when the habits of people's eyes are uncovered, the press could be summoned to shape the public mind. The common thought process in America was that fact-based journalism was the chief means of persuasion in our culture. Lippmann determined that the press would be the shaper of public opinion, and public opinions would be organized for the press. The political science of the press shaping public opinion was called "perception management."[19] Lippmann turned to Hollywood for their use of images and pictures to persuade and sway public consciousness. Significant steps were being taken down the road of the idolatrous and diabolical imagination because not only were appeals to reason discarded as futile, they were also undercut to serve the interests of power. Lippmann, without qualification or equivocation, abandoned the idea of meaningful public dialogue. It is here that the idolatrous and the diabolical imagination are revealed in Lippmann's thinking. For Lippman, it was not that people could not rationally deliberate the issues, it was that the time required for rational deliberations obstructed the efficient exercise of executive power. Thus executive power must use symbols because symbols provided a vehicle to overcome the inconviences of critical reason and public discussion. The articulated and intentional absence of critical reason and rational discussion is evidence of the idolatrous and diabolical imagination.

For Lippmann, and subsequently Bernays, the manipulation and facilitation of carefully chosen images, symbols, and pictures bridged the aspirations of participation of the public with needs of the elite to govern swiftly and effectively. The critical task of leadership is to create, manage, and project images and signposts to most efficiently guide the public mind. One final quote in the attempt to discuss the rootage of the contemporary idolatrous and diabolical imagination:

---

19. Ibid., 151.

Lippmann saw the strategic employment of media images as the secret to modern power, the means by which leaders and special interests might cloak themselves in the "fiction" that they stand as delegates of the common good. The most compelling attribute of symbols, he asserted, was the capacity to magnify emotion while undermining critical thought, to emphasize sensations while subverting ideas. "In the symbol," he rhapsodized, "emotion is discharged at a common target and the idiosyncrasy of real ideas is blotted out."[20]

The one who captures the symbols of public feeling controls the formation and delivery of public policy. This Lippmann coined as the "manufacturing of consent."

Though Bernays carefully subscribed to and followed Lippmann's work, he considered it too academic because Lipmann never got down to the practical work of the changing of public opinion. For example, in 1947, Bernays offered practical application of Lippman's concept, "manufacturing of consent," by authoring an important essay titled, "The Engineering of Consent."[21] Bernays was determined to apply Lippman's principles and "engineer" the public mind to consent. As part of this application, while most publicists saw their work as writing and distributing press releases and facilitating press conferences, Bernays saw the role as invisibly and clandestinely staging "events" (see hotel example in the last section) that the press would cover on the publicists' terms out of habit. Bernays discarded the term "press agent," and referred to himself as "counsel on public relations." Bernays described "counsel on public relations" as one who would prescribe for a client the most effective ways to navigate an increasingly complicated, often hostile, social environment.[22] Following Lippmann, Bernays saw the "counsel on public relations" as one of the intelligent elite who had the skills to negotiate the democratic aspirations of the masses of citizens and necessities of elite power. To direct the masses, ruling elites would subject the masses to a scientifically informed tool:

---

20. Ibid., 157.

21. Edward L. Bernays, "The Engineering of Consent," *The Annals of the American Academy of Political and Social Science* 250 (March 1947): 113–20, http://journals.sagepub.com/doi/abs/10.1177/000271624725000116.

22. Ewen, 163.

propaganda. He even called propaganda "the executive arm of the invisible government."[23] Bernays set standards and practices that would blossom into many of the practices used today in the idolatrous and diabolical imagination to shape the public mind in regard to politics, economics, and even the church. In some instances, like the press, the church can be an invaluable and necessary conduit of the propaganda of the ruling elite, if not an outright support, through its complicity in silence. Bernays practiced propaganda as public submission, the attempt for the public to comprehend the world in the propagandist's desired way.

Again, following Lipmann, Bernays realized that to forge public opinion, the propagandist must forego all attempts to reason with the public:

> Abstract discussions and heavy facts…cannot be given to the public until they are simplified and dramatized. Bernays designated this propagandist version of reality "news." When reality is distilled down to its most "simplified and dramatized" form and is able to make an appeal to the instincts of the public mind—"it can be aptly termed news. And the public relations counsel created news."[24]

Much like the challenge that confronts our nation in the presidency of Donald J. Trump, Bernays developed and normalized a great transformation in the way that society defined information. According to Ewen,

> If at the turn of the century, "news" had been understood as a faithful extension of an *objective* world. Bernays approached "news" as an essentially subjective category, something that took place, and could be generated—in the pliant minds of the audience at whom a parcel of information was being directed. If news had once been understood as something out there, waiting to be covered, now it was seen as product to be manufactured, something designated and transmitted to bring about a visceral public response.[25]

For the propagandist, fake news, alternative facts, alternative information, and even alternative history are necessary for executive action. As a matter

---

23. Edward Bernays, *Propaganda* (New York: Routledge, 1928), 48.

24. Ewen, 171.

25. Ibid.

of practice, I consider any information disseminated from the Trump administration as propaganda, until verified and proven otherwise.

Bernays believed that given the scale of modern democratic society and its need for communication infrastructure, the need to "engineer consent" had become a necessary precondition for the exercise of power. The leader, using communication infrastructure, garners support for their ideas and programs by the manufacturing and engineering consent.

Bernays realized that these techniques could be used for "possible evil" or anti-democratic purposes. Bernays was shocked that Joseph Gobbels was using his book *Crystallizing Public Opinion* as a basis for the destructive campaign against the Jews of Germany. Though Bernays offered lip service to the democratic ideal of a body of informed citizens, he still fundamentally practiced and believed that leadership could not be effective without the engineering of consent. In some ways, I understand Bernays's point. I have been a pastor, a religious leader, and I have had to manufacture consent to gain support for "God's ideas and programs." I would hope that, most of the time, I utilized this manufactured consent toward good ends that serve God and help people. But, the question must be asked: How do we guard against the inevitable temptation to use these skills for our own benefit? When we use these skills toward our own benefit, we develop the mentality that I once heard put like this: "The enemies of our privilege are construed as the enemies of humanity." How do we know that we will not manufacture consent to that which will benefit primarily us? Might I ask, do we have to manufacture consent for God's agenda? I think we do, but how do we guard against the tendency to believe that which will benefit us? This is why it is important that truth be outside of our subjective reality as corrective of our subjective propaganda. This is why objective facts, accountability, and reality connected to the wisdom of the ages matter.

These techniques and the assumptions behind them of Lippmann and Bernays can easily become by their very nature anti-democratic. They function out of the idolatrous and diabolical imagination and are contrary to the moral imagination. They could be used for good, but often the temptation to manipulation based upon the paternalism and intellectual arrogance of assuming that one knows what is best for a group comes to destructive ends. The wisdom of the ages has taught human beings that absolute power corrupts absolutely. Also, the maneuvering and exploitation of truth for one's own purposes facilitates outright lies, further undercutting the moral fabric of democracy and community.

Specifically, the fourth question of the moral imagination must be asked: Is engineering consent consistent with the language of poetry and art that lifts and elevates the human spirit by touching the emotive chords of wonder, hope, and mystery? I answer definitely not, and therefore as I view it, Donald J. Trump and most of the Republican leadership that colludes with him do not operate out of the highest ideals of the moral imagination. A new kind of moral leadership is needed, a moral leadership consistent with the four qualities of the moral imagination. Let me quickly present one vision of moral leadership.

A Vision of Moral Leadership

Dov Seidman, author, businessman, and generative moral thought-leader made interesting comments in reference to moral imagination as necessary for moral leadership. At the Davos World Economic Forum Annual Meeting 2017, on a panel titled, "The Great American Divide," he asked this question in response to being asked the question of the possibility of American unity after the 2016 presidential election: "Are we divided or are we being divided?"[26] He suggested that with cheap, ubiquitous, and easy-to-use tools of division, such as Twitter, that undermining unity was so common that it is difficult to even find a way to disagree respectfully, let alone accomplish unity. He suggested that elections are contests of candidates, platforms, and visions, but the 2016 American presidential election was an election of protest. Sixty percent of the electorate wanted to disrupt, not just Washington, but also "the system," (i.e., capitalism,

---

26. "The Great American Divide with Hamza Yusuf," Davos World Economic Forum Annual Meeting 2017, *YouTube*, January 20, 2017, https://www.youtube.com/watch?v=uge3NuBHCuA; "Dov Seidman at the 2016 Fortune-Time Global Forum," *Fortune + Time Global Forum Rome 2016 Fortune Magazine* (December 2, 2016), https://www.youtube.com/watch?v=B2ZqEBLk1-8.

the economy—"the whole thing") because they believed "the system was rigged." Compounding the problem was within communication structures an "industry of anger," where money is being made whipping up people into a frenzy of outrage. It was clear to him that America was not divided, but that it was being divided by communication tools of division and profits of the industry of outrage. At the time of Sideman's speaking, he was not able to address the now-proven notion that Russia and Russian operatives attempted to stoke division through the use of targeted and specific social media ads in the attempt to influence the presidential election. Americans were being divided by the global sabatoge of a foreign government.

He noted that the fundamental values of America were liberty and freedom. Across the globe and in America as well there was a lack, an inequality of income and inequality of freedom. Technological forces were creating an abundance of "freedom from," a massive casting off of authority, truth, decency, micromanaging bosses, institutions, or anything that attempts to control or define us. For example, he mentioned that Uber was casting off the taxicab industry, and Amazon was casting of the big-box stores. The spirit of the age was the casting off of all authority, what he called "freedom from" based in technological innovation and the culture of outrage.

According to Seidman, America was not just "freedom from," but more importantly "freedom to." America was freedom to pursue a meaningful and happy life, freedom to express oneself, and the freedom to pursue the America Dream. But, there is a scarcity of "freedom to" in America. There is plenty of "freedom from" but little understanding of "freedom to."

Seidman maintains that philosopher David Hume reasoned that the moral imagination diminishes with distance.[27] As distance increases

---

27. Hume argues that human beings are strongly governed by the imagination. Imagination is responsible for both the individual human mind and social arrangements that human beings form collectively. Concerning each individual mind, Hume argues that the imagination explains how we form "abstract" or "general" ideas; how we reason from causes to their effects, or from effects to their causes; why we tend to sympathize, or share the feelings of other people; why we project some of our feelings onto objects in the world around us, and the numerous "fictions" that we believe. Concerning human social arrangements, he argues that the imagination explains why we form governments, and shape the laws that we adopt, including those that govern the distribution of property and the passage of national authority from one leader to the next. In Hume's view, to "sympathize" is to share the feelings of a person whom one

between people, the moral imagination decreases, hence less sympathy and more outrage. Seidman suggests that we live in a "no distance" world, and it leads quickly to moral arousal (outrage), and we are outraged, we are more focused on "freedom from," or casting off, rather than "freedom to." In this state of moral arousal, the tendency is to skip conversation and dialogue, and go right to resolution, such as "fire the bums," "take the name off the building," or "lock her up." The opposite of moral arousal is moral progress, and where there is moral progress, there is nuance, equanimity, patience, deliberation, multiple conversations, and patient dialogue. But in the culture of outrage, there is little of the nuance of morality. The one who is outraged demands immediate relief. This is not to say that some forms of oppression and violence warrant outrage and immediate relief, but it is always wise to remember that the ultimate truth is always the domain of nuance and the discussion, and is connected to the wisdom of the ages. When we "throw the bums out," we get resolution, but make no moral progress. As an example, for seven years before and during the 2016 presidential campaign, Donald Trump and Republicans operated, fostered, and endorsed a culture of outrage in regard to the Affordable Care Act (Obamacare) through shouts of "repeal and replace" and negative bluster. When they came to power through these means of propaganda, it was time to reveal their plan. They discovered that it would have been better to approach health care, even a system that one wants to repeal, with nuance, meaningful dialogue, and conversation. It would be helpful to discuss, for example, how many people were receiving life-saving healthcare. Instead, nearly all Republicans demonized the Affordable Care Act, whipping people up into a frenzy of outrage. When their constituents discovered what benefits and coverage they would lose, Republicans had no flexibility. After several years of calling for repeal and replacement, when they finally had the muscle with majorities in the Senate, House, and the Presidency,

---

encounters. Hume argues that moral sentiments—the approval that we feel when considering someone's virtues, and the disapproval when considering vices, derive from sympathy. As people become more distant from each other in space and time, ideas of them and their passions become less strongly associated with our forceful and vivacious perceptions of ourselves; we therefore sympathize less strongly with them (*Internet Encyclopedia of Philosophy*, "David Hume: Imagination," accessed August 31, 2017, http://www.iep.utm.edu/hume-ima/#SH4c).

they had no alternative plan for healthcare in America. They had no "freedom to." When we operate out of dystopian moral outrage, we will have a clear view of what we believe is wrong, but have no vision from moral imagination of the future to which we aspire, other than "throw the bums out" or "repeal and replace." At the time of this writing, President Trump has decided to dismantle the Affordable Care Act with Executive Action without any plan for replacement, other than placing the matter in the hands of Congress. Seidman argues for a new kind of moral leadership.

Though formal authority has been disrupted by ubiquitous communication through technological change, most of the leadership in our time is based in formal authority. Formal authority is authority because you were elected or appointed to a position, or because you are the boss or the parent. In this age, title does not automatically mean authority. Formal authority says, "Do this because I said so," or "because I am your parent," or "because I am the boss." For Seidman, and I agree, in our technological age, the only true authority is moral authority:

> Moral authority is the ability to elevate people with visions that inspire them to go on a journey worthy of their dedication. Moral leadership is inspirational leadership, the ability to connect with people around values, beliefs, missions and purposes worthy of their collective efforts.[28]

Moral authority is in scarce supply in our country and world. It takes moral authority to do big things together, such as healthcare in America. The question must be asked: When was the last time America did anything big together? From Seidman's perspective, only moral authority can bring us together. Who is the moral leader of our nation? Who can bring us together to accomplish the big things to make life better for all?

"Freedom to" involves the issue of trust, where people either affirm or disappoint trust, but the issue is trust. Trust builds capacity and innovation, and maximizes the contribution of all in the home, workplace, country, and the world. A lack of trust is at the heart of the

---

28. Dov Seidman, "From Formal Authority to Moral Authority," *Faith and Leadership*, October 8, 2012, https://www.faithandleadership.com/qa/dov-seidman-formal-authority-moral-authority?page=full.

opinion-management philosophy of Lippman and Bernays. The common people cannot be trusted so the role of the counselor is to manage the dialectic of the democratic aspirations of common people with the needs of the elite to make efficient decisions. Spin, fake news, alternative facts, and fake history are necessary. Leadership with such tools is the kind of leadership that does not inspire us to a journey worthy of our dedication. To go on a journey worthy of our dedication involves honesty, transparency, accountability, and character. This kind of moral leadership is deeply aligned with the wisdom of the ages, and the four moral qualities discussed herein.

Finally, who is the moral leader of our nation? Seidman says, referring to Donald J. Trump that we have a "bully in the bully pulpit, and we will see if formal leadership can still work."[29] From my social location, it is not working and will not work because the dystopian nature of the idolatrous and diabolical imagination is not the language of poetry and art that lifts and elevates by touching the emotive chords of wonder, hope, and mystery. Dystopian language is great for people who are in outrage and want to disrupt and tear things up, but it will rarely do anything meaningful that is large and lasting because its tendency is to blame and scapegoat, to do violence, to operate in division and hatred, and to tear things up with no plan for the future. The future is always in the language of poetry and art that lifts and elevates by touching the chords of mystery, wonder, and hope. The future is in these four characteristics of moral authority.

Ultimately, we cannot languish in singularly lamenting the absence of moral leadership; it is our responsibility to provide the moral leadership from our moral imagination that is missing. It is our responsibility to protest, march, vote, write books, and in this instance preach, in whatever form of resistance that is operative in our moral imagination; but these must engage, act upon, and lift up the fourth quality of moral imagination: the language of poetry and art that lifts and elevates by touching the emotive chords of wonder, hope, and mystery. This is the responsibility of the church and our preaching. In the next chapter, I will talk about

---

29. "The Great American Divide with Hamza Yusuf."

the four qualities of moral imagination in our preaching. Let me refresh your memory again: *preaching from moral imagination is the ability of the preacher, intuitive or otherwise, in the midst of the chaotic experiences of life and existence, to grasp and share God's abiding wisdom and ethical truth in order to benefit the individual and common humanity.*

HOW TO PREACH A DANGEROUS SERMON:

FOUR QUALITIES OF MORAL IMAGINATION IN A SERMON

Unless theology begins with the sharecropper... not just the shopper,
it's nothing but a heap of words. The games people play....

Frederick Herzog

You will remember that back in chapter 1, "Race, Shrinking White-ness, and Four Qualities of the Moral Imagination of Robert F. Kennedy," I discussed the concept that not all whites have benefited equally from white supremacy, hence the phenomenon of "shrinking whiteness." Large numbers of white people do not have access to "whiteness." Thomas Piketty suggests the source is "patrimonial capitalism" and cites as evidence that from 1977–2007, 60 percent of the total increase of the national income of America went to the top 1 percent. As wealth accumulates in fewer and fewer hands, the few, by virtue of vast sums of wealth, can buy the political system and establish governance that primarily protects and advances their interests. It is clear that the rich have disproportionate power over politics, government, and society. This has always been the case, but this stark and blunt reality was overwhelmingly apparent based upon closer investigations of the housing and banking crash of 2007–2009 and the Great Recession. The ability of the few to prosper regardless of circumstances, often at the expense of the many, led to the 2016 presidential election becoming, in the words of Dov Seidman, a "protest election." Sixty percent of the electorate wanted to disrupt, not just Washington, but also "the system," because "the system was rigged." For much of the history of black and brown America, the system has always been "rigged," but the massive inequality of wealth, and subsequently the inequality of freedom, made it apparent that many whites have also been excluded. This, of course, is not a new reality, but the indoctrination and subsequent loss of the narrative of the American Dream makes for large measures of white disillusionment and anger. If Trump was effective at speaking to and for white anger, where was the church as a countervailing voice leading people to more positive responses and hopeful directions? What hope did the white church have to offer to the crisis of the loss of the narrative of the American Dream? How does the white church, and the black church for that matter, speak to the onslaught of the idolatrous and diabolical imagination in American culture? Following Ruby Sales, I suggested that we needed a white liberation theology, and specifically a white liberation theology that takes seriously the parameters of the four qualities of the moral imagination. We need theology that addresses the American domination narrative of the idolatrous and diabolical imagination.

In light of all of the above, the question remains: How do we preach the gospel of Jesus Christ in this oppressive cultural context? How do we preach freedom and equality for all, the four qualities of the moral imagination, in the face of such a massive and glittering commitment to the idolatrous and diabolical imagination? In this chapter, I will flesh out how to preach a sermon from the moral imagination. I will include a homiletic method that includes the four qualities of the moral imagination, and speaks to a vision of freedom and equality for all.

I was provided a platform from which to launch this chapter by a person who astutely responded to a lecture that I delivered. This "friendly responder" provided feedback and offered a response to each of the four qualitlies of the moral imagination. He suggested that his comments were "anti-moral imagination."

Perspectives of the Anti-Moral Imagination

I delivered a lecture at a gathering, based in the concept of "The Wisdom of the Ages," from this book. I began the lecture by listing the four qualities of the moral imagination. An audience member, whom I will call "Friendly Responder," quickly wrote a response to each quality that he called in his comments, the perspective of the "anti-moral imagination." Speaking from the context of the white church in America, an assessment was offered as to why the average white church departed so far from the four qualities of the moral imagination that I offered. The reflections were so powerful that I would like to list a summary of his comment to each of the four qualities. But first, it would be helpful to understand the background and context of Friendly Responder.

Friendly Responder is a pastor and said in remarks that he had come from a family with a long history of cross-cultural negotiations. His wife was also a pastor and served a congregation where Chrysler's factory pull-out cut the town population in half. Years of high-paying jobs with little education left the town with a less-than-mobile work force and no jobs. Those who could afford to leave and were educated enough to find a new career did so. But many were stuck. There were many stories of loss and frustration in her church, and the same story was repeated in smaller towns across the rural areas where they both frequently preached. Along the way, he began to wrestle with their "narrative." Even though he grew up as the son of a steel worker, he recognized the way they saw the world was very different.

Friendly Responder recounted that while doing an interim pastor position at a church, he had a great conversation with one of the more conservative elders. The elder was concerned about Friendly Responder pushing an anti-racism curriculum for a church study. They were able to talk about white privilege in honest ways. The elder was offended by the amount of guilt he perceived in the issue. When Friendly Responder suggested that it was more about responsibility than guilt, he opened up about his own feelings of helplessness. Friendly Responder reported that it took some time, but the elder eventually realized that much of the "guilt" was his own assumptions rather than what others were saying. Friendly Responder reported wishing that he had more time to talk with him because his belief was that the real issue was fear, specifically fear of a changing American narrative. In my estimation, this fear of a changing American narrative echoes what Paul Krugman said in response to the Anne Case and Sir Angus Deaton report, "Rising morbidity and mortality in midlife among white non-Hispanic Americans in the 21st century," that we discussed in chapter 1. You will remember Krugman said, "we are looking at people who were raised to believe in the American Dream, and are coping badly with its failure to come true."

In our follow-up correspondence, Friendly Responder identified what he believed was the narrative of the white church. He said it is a 1980s blending of patriotism and faith. A narrative of entitlement that white America has "worked for" as each generation leaves something for those who follow. Within this narrative of entitlement, people feel like they (or their family) earned their place and status. If the "work hard" portion of the American Dream seems to have been lost along the way, it was paid for in the past, so it is still the expectation now. It is not only expected, but also justified by hard work, patriotic duty, loyalty, and faithfulness to God. Reporting without judgment, he suggested that it's a wrapping of Christian faith up in morality laws and American cultural norms. I translate these cultural norms as the idolatrous and diabolical imagination.

Friendly Responder emphasized that there is a sincerity of faith involved here. These are good folks and not bad people. There might be inaccurate theology and bad leadership in the face of success, but there is real faith and a real relationship with Jesus. Let's look at his response to the four qualities. To remind ourselves, let me again list the four qualities of moral imagination:

1. Envision equality and represent it by one's physical presence

2. Empathy as a catalyst or bridge to create opportunities to overcome the past and make new decisions for peace and justice

3. Wisdom and truth in ancient texts, the wisdom of the ages

4. The language of poetry and art that lifts and elevates by touching the emotive chords of wonder, hope, and mystery

Anti-Moral Imagination Response to the Four Qualities of Moral Imagination

Here are the comments of Friendly Responder (in italics) to each of the four qualities of the moral imagination.

Envision equality and represent that by one's physical presence

An older woman told me about the historic lack of tension in town between blacks and whites. She said: "I had black friends and they never expressed any concern to me." I remember the confusion on her face when I asked, "Why do you think they would confide in you if they felt uncomfortable?" I also remember the honesty in a young black man in my congregation who talked to me about what he sacrificed in his soul to live as a star athlete and publicly embraced minority in that town. We take the acquaintances we have with people of color and exaggerate the trust and openness. We feel comfortable telling them how we feel and they don't contradict or complain, so everything must be fine. It is an assumption born of privilege and theo-political narrative. We fixed it in the 60s, and we all walked hand in hand, so we are all good now; and don't challenge that narrative or you will be seen as a trouble maker.

Empathy as a catalyst or bridge to create opportunities to overcome the past and make new decisions for peace and justice

Beyond the death of Jesus as sacrifice, there is the sacrifice of generations before us and our military service men (and women) who have earned our freedom and security in this theo-political narrative. Somehow, we have moved from a call to risk and sacrifice to justified stability and security. We think being faithful protects us from harm rather than calling us to race into trouble in the name of God. A friend at a theological seminary worked on a "Youth Spirituality Project." In his conversations with parents, he gleaned a common expectation and desire for church ministry with youth: "Teach them to be nice and safe." This desire goes directly against the idea of suffering as a path to wisdom and scripture, but it is appealing.

Wisdom and truth in ancient texts: The wisdom of the ages

A good word pairing that rings true here is nostalgic and domesticated. Many think the "ancient" wisdom isn't deep or ancient enough. We look at the sacrifice of our grandparents, especially the Word War II generation and let the romanticized version of their sacrifice grant authority to our morality. We celebrate their sacrifice and talk about returning to such a world, such a time and place without being willing to even consider the sacrifice required or the brokenness that was also part of their lives. Going back even further and digging deeper challenges our narrative, so we draw dividing lines in history that give us permission to ignore what came before. We are post-reformation, post-revolution, post-civil war, etc. We "arrived" in those moments and claim the victor's right to dictate the narrative. We glorify that past time, allowing it to justify our sinful lack of perspective in the present and future. Deep wisdom goes beyond our narrative and looks at the whole people of God. We have to allow the faith journey of others to critique our perspective without dismissing it or getting angry about it. Unfortunately, the diversity to explore such deep wisdom is all around us, but we keep the Church as homogenous as possible.

The language of poetry and art that lifts and elevates by touching the emotive chords of wonder, hope, and mystery

I experience the modern church, especially the white church as being anti-mystery, preferring concrete behaviors and morality codes by which to judge our faithfulness. Yet, when a contradiction pops up in scripture, or a disconnect between our homogenized faith narrative and the Gospels, we chalk it up to mystery and say that "all things are possible" in Christ. I see a similar response to art: we seem to be overwhelmed by shallow such as "Chicken-soup for the Soul" books, poems, and slogans, often with pretty pictures of creation in the background. Art that challenges or upsets us is dismissed as inappropriate. The advantage of living with privilege is that you dictate the narrative, and we have domesticated our faith narrative till it often fails to reflect our Lord.

I am deeply appreciative of this anti-moral imagination feedback, even though it is the reflections of only one person. It helped me to understand, in some measure, why the white evangelical church voted over 80 percent for Trump in the 2016 presidential election. I was struck by several overall generalizations that form a domesticated and nostalgic theo-political narrative based in the idolatrous and diabolical imagination to support and continually justify Trump's presidency and white supremacy. Based in the victor's right to declare the narrative, the faith journeys of others are not allowed to critique this theo-political, idolatrous, and diabolical narrative. To avoid the exploration of such wisdom, the goal is to keep the church as homogenous as possible. Components of the theo-political narrative are, first, the exaggeration of relationships of trust and openness with people of color based in the white American narrative that things were fixed in the 1960s and are fine now. Second, the abandonment of risk and sacrifice for the nation or the gospel of Jesus Christ is based in the romantization of the sacrifice of generations making it possible for the present generation to enjoy stability and security. Third, the overwhelming majority of the white church is seeking to return to the world shaped and provided by the sacrifices of the World War II generation without even considering the sacrifices or real brokenness that were a part of their lives. Finally, the focus is anti-mystery, preferring concrete behaviors and morality codes as the measure of faithfulness. Overwhelmed with the shallowness of books, poems, slogans, and the like, there is the refusal of any art that challenges or upsets. In summary, the church based in the cultural norms of the idolatrous and diabolical imagination support the champion of idolatrous and diabolical imagination norms (Trump), even when the norms and behaviors are inconsistent with the gospel of Jesus Christ, including racism, sexual assault of women, and lying (to only name a few). I believe that preaching the four aspects of the moral imagination is dangerous in the cultural context of this theo-political narrative.

A Brief Homiletic Method for Preaching Moral Imagination

In a very brief way, I want to look at the preparation of a sermon that intentionally includes the four qualities of the moral imagination. From the perspective of method, I would like to demonstrate to the reader how to prepare a sermon that incorporates the moral imagination. Then, I will present a sermon entitled "Did Heaven Make a Mistake?" based on Lamentatins 3:20-23 (NIV):

> And my soul is downcast within me. Yet this I call to mind and therefore I have hope: Because of the LORD's great love we are not consumed, for his compassions never fail. They are new every morning; great is your faithfulness.

In my preaching textbook, *They Like to Never Quit Praisin' God: The Role of Celebration in Preaching*, and accompanying workbook, *Preaching as Celebration Digital Lecture Series and Workbook*, I advocate an experiential preaching preparation process.[1] While this is not the best space

---

1. Frank A. Thomas, *They Like to Never Quit Praisin' God: The Role of Celebration in Preaching* (Cleveland: Pilgrim Press, 2013) and Thomas, *Preaching as Celebration Digital Lecture Series and Workbook* (Indianapolis: Hope for Life, Inc. Press, 2014).

to go into those details because the reader can locate these for further study, it is important to highlight the overall steps in the Spirit-aided experiential sermon preparation process: prayer, free association, exegesis, development of the Preaching Worksheet, and the writing and delivery of the sermon.

The Preaching Worksheet functions to synthesize the accumulated information and develop a behavioral purpose statement for the sermon. The behavioral purpose statement is the mission statement, or the guiding declaration, of the sermon. The preacher clearly identifies the message of the sermon and the behavioral purpose to which they will call the people in response to what the preacher has said. Again, please see the aforementioned book and workbook for more detail.

Preaching Worksheet

1. What does this passage say to me?

2. What does this passage say to the needs of people in our time?

3. What is the "bad news" in the text? What is the "bad news" for our time?

4. What is the "good news" in the text? What is the "good news" for our time?

5. Behavioral Purpose Statement

6. Strategy for Celebration

   What shall we celebrate?
   How shall we celebrate our response in 6a?
   What materials of celebration shall we use?

With the Preaching Worksheet fully fleshed out, the preacher's next step in the experiential sermon preparation process is to structure the sermon. Many think of the structure of a sermon as its inductive or deductive flow. I organize the sermon in an inductive flow around four very simple questions in discussion with the text and context:

1. What is the situation? (Preaching Worksheet Questions 1 and 2)
2. What is the complication? (Preaching Worksheet Question 3)
3. What is the resolution? (Preaching Worksheet Question 4)
4. What is the celebration? (Preaching Worksheet Question 6)

The responses to these questions flow from the Preaching Worksheet. The preacher develops the sermon into its best-written expression and prepares for the delivery of the sermon. Again, much more detail about the experiential sermon preparation process is available specifically in both *They Like to Never Quit Praisin' God: The Role of Celebration in Preaching* and *Preaching as Celebration Digital Lecture Series and Workbook.*[2]

In the case of preaching from the moral imagination, I would suggest adding one more step. I suggest that after completing the Preaching Worksheet the preacher take one more step. Before the preacher writes the sermon,[3] the preacher would respond to five questions:

1. Where in this text do we find equality envisioned and represented by physical presence?

2. Where in this text do we notice empathy as a catalyst or bridge to create opportunities to overcome the past and make new decisions for peace and justice?

3. Where do we find wisdom and truth in this ancient text, the wisdom of the ages?

4. Where is the language of poetry and art that lifts and elevates by touching the emotive chords of wonder, hope, and mystery?

5. To what contemporary moral concern would you apply your responses in these four questions?

---

2. Thomas, "Designing for Celebration," *They Like to Never Quit Praisin' God*, 71–106; Thomas, "The Experiential Preaching Process," *Preaching as Celebration*, 54–67. (Lectures on digital files included.)

3. The five questions of the moral imagination not only flow with the celebrative preaching method but can be added to any method, including the Four Pages, Conversational Approach to Preaching, Expository Preaching, or Hegelian Method of Samuel DeWitt Proctor.

Behavorial Purpose Statement for Lamentations 3:20-23

I propose to experientially demonstrate that God's steadfast love in Lamentations 3:20-23 sustains the world and overcomes Jeremiah's despair to the end that those who work for a moral world would overcome despair and find wonder, mystery, and hope in the love of God.

Five Questions of the Moral Imagination for Lamentations 3:20-23

I turn now to my responses to the five questions of the four qualities of the moral imagination in regard to our text, Lamentations 3:20-23.

Where in this text do we find equality envisioned and represented by physical presence?

The incarnation of God's *hesed* (faithfulnes and love) is the ultimate act of generosity and love: that God would locate Godself in human form to prop the world up and save humankind from its lack of morality. This love inspires and calls Christians to be God's *hesed* and prop the world up with acts of love and kindness and protest injustice.

Where in this text do we notice empathy as a catalyst or bridge to create opportunities to overcome the past and make new decisions for peace and justice?

God's *hesed* came in Jesus and propped the world up, and that generous compassion gives us the opportunity for empathy to overcome the past and make new decisions for peace and justice. For example, after the assassination of police officers in Brooklyn, the wife of Eric Garner exhibited empathy and made a new decision of peace and justice in laying a wreath at the grave of the fallen officers, even though her husband died in a chokehold by police.

Where do we find wisdom and truth in this ancient text, the wisdom of the ages?

The wisdom of ages is the very words of the text itself: "Because of the LORD's great love we are not consumed, for his compassions never fail. They are new every morning; great is your faithfulness." God's love for humankind will never end. God will never abandon the quest for justice, mercy, and peace.

Where is the language of poetry and art that lifts and elevates by touching the emotive chords of wonder, hope, and mystery?

The resolution of the prophet Jeremiah's despair at the conditions and destruction of Israel based in the love of God is uplifting and elevating. There are times in life where we experience the despair Jeremiah articulates. But Jeremiah discovers and gives witness to the faithful love of God, which stirs the chords of wonder, mystery, and hope in him and us. The steadfast love of the Lord never ceases; it is new every morning.

To what contemporary moral concern would you apply your responses in these four questions of the four qualities of the moral imagination?

In the age of Trump's presidential leadership, for many who work for social justice and improving social conditions, a kind of despair can be overwhelming. Many activists recognize what they are doing as good, true, and significant, but they are working against the way things fundamentally are in life, and it causes in them a kind of despair. Human beings are, for example, fundamentally tribal and self-preserving; and to improve things, people are asked to be unselfish, to be concerned with someone outside their group, persons who would be considered their sisters and brothers. The sermon seeks to allow the love of God to address this despair in activists and create more activists.

Once the Five Questions of the Moral Imagination have been completed, then the preacher begins to draft the sermon. With the experiential sermon preparation process completed and when several drafts of the sermon have been produced, one is ready for the preaching of the sermon.

Moral Versus Political

It is important to distinguish what is "moral" and what is "political." Preachers often get accused of being "political" in the pulpit, and as a result many shy away from moral preaching. There is a difference between moral issues and political issues, though moral issues can be made political. My father fell ill and was in intensive care for thirty days. My seventy-eight-year-old dad lay there worried about the cost of treatment and whether or not the costs would financially wipe out their nest egg that they had spent an entire lifetime gathering. The bill for his care was over $350,000. This was not a chronic illness but one medical emergency that turned into thirty days of crisis in intensive care and almost killed him from an infection he picked up in the hospital. Fortunately enough, he lived and the majority of the medical bills were covered with health insurance.

Healthcare is a moral issue because of all that my mother and father had contributed to this country as fine, upstanding citizens by voting, paying taxes, working, contributing to the economy, and being honest and decent people for over seventy-eight years of life. It would be a crime, in a nation with all this wealth, to allow them to lose their entire life savings over one medical emergency. This is also a moral issue based on my reading of scripture and discerning of faith and vision for the reign of God in the world. Every person is created equal in the image of God and in God's reign of love, truth, and justice. As such, people would have food for their stomachs, education for their brains, hope for their hearts, and healthcare for their bodies. This is what I envision as the reign of God in my moral imagination. And once we settle the issue that healthcare is a moral issue, then we can settle the political and fiscal will to make it happen. I would be willing to sacrifice and pay an amount in extra taxes to ensure that this loss of life savings would not occur to my parents or any other parents living in this nation. I would pay taxes for people to have the opportunity of healthcare. This for me is fundamentally a moral issue, an issue of being humane one to another. I do not allow people to make it a political issue between Democrats, Independents, and Republicans. I argue this: preach the moral base of issues, and though you will be accused of preaching politics, you will in fact be preaching dangerous sermons. Preaching healthcare for all, at least in some communities, is a dangerous sermon. Preaching about the care and concern of God's green earth is a dangerous sermon. Preaching about white supremacy and white privilege is a dangerous sermon. This is not to suggest that every sermon that is preached is to be a dangerous sermon, but at least some of the sermons one preaches should be dangerous.

A SERMON OF THE MORAL IMAGINATION: "DID HEAVEN MAKE A MISTAKE?"

Witnessing all of the injustice, hate, violence, and cruelty; the hurt and the pain caused in this world by human beings upon other human beings. Witnessing the levels of rape, misogyny, molestations, abuse of women, human and girl trafficking, discrimination against the LGBTQ community, the economic and political exploitation of the poor, the white supremacy, xenophobia, racism and prejudice against minorities and immigrants, the inequality between the rich and the poor, the devastation of the environment, what Pope Francis calls "our common home"—and most of it perpetrated in the name of God and high-minded democratic ideals. Witnessing the drug trafficking, the continual and repetitive shooting of unarmed African American men and women, the mass incarceration of black people, racial profiling, along with the justifications, denials, and defense of state-sponsored terrorism. Witnessing the assassination of police officers and hearing the blind and tribal defense of guns in our gun-crazed world and glorification of violence culture. Witnessing the abandonment of the right of healthcare for all. I have come to the conclusion that though from Genesis 1:26 we claim to be above and have dominion over the animals, the fact is that we really are animals— animals trying to be moral or what one writer calls "moral animals."[4] We are trying to be moral, but when you scratch us or we perceive that we—or our interests—are threatened, we go straight to our instincts as animals. We are really animals trying to be moral. I wonder if human beings deserve to be created. With Sandy Eisenberg Sasso, I ask the question: "Do humans deserve the gift of life?" Did heaven make a mistake?[5]

In Sasso's book *Midrash: Reading the Bible with Question Marks*, she records several stories of Rabbis debating this very difficult question:

> Rabbi Simon said: When the Holy One, the blessed one, came to create the Adam, the ministering angels formed themselves into groups and parties, some of them saying, "Let the human be created," while others urged, "Let the human not be created."... The Angel of Love said, "Let humans be created, because they will dispense acts of love"; Angel of Truth said, "Let humans not be created, because they will speak falsehood." The Angel of Righteousness said, "Let humans be created, because they will perform righteous deeds"; the Angel of Peace said, "Let human beings not be

---

4. Robert Wright, *The Moral Animal: Evolutionary Psychology and Everyday Life* (New York: Vintage Books, 1994).

5. Sandy Eisenberg Sasso, *Midrash: Reading the Bible with Question Marks* (Brewster, MA: Paraclete Press, 2013), "Should Humans Have Been Created?" 52–65.

91

created, because they are full of strife." What did
the Lord do? The Lord took Truth and cast it to
the ground. Said the ministering angels before the
Holy One: "Sovereign of the Universe! Why do you
despise your seal? Let truth arise from the earth!"[6]

The rabbis are doing a riff on the *we* in let *us* create in
Genesis 1:26. The rabbis in this story suggest that "let us"
means that God consulted the angels about the creation
of humanity. Rabbi Simon sees angels arguing with themselves. The Angel of Love favors creation because humans will act lovingly. The Angel of Truth objects because
humans will tell lies. The Angel of Righteousness gives the
nod of assent because they will perform good deeds. The
Angel of Peace claims that human beings are full of strife.
The vote is tied two angels to two angels, and God has to
break the tie. God decides by throwing the Angel of Truth
out of heaven and casting Truth to the ground.

It is not that the Angel of Truth is incorrect in assess-
ing human character; it is that God wants to create despite the fact that humans will lie and contend with each
other. The angels take no comfort in God's action, and
the angel chorus says, "Let Truth spring up from the earth
and return to its proper place in the heavens!" But God
pays no attention because if Truth assumed its proper
place, human beings could not exist.

This story through the rabbis tells us something about
their profound disappointment in human beings and human behavior and their almost despair that we will ever
change. It takes overwhelming disappointment to question whether or not God should have created us in the
first place. That is where I am right now. I am profoundly
disappointed, profoundly hurt, and profoundly angry.
I had hoped that with the 2008 and 2012 election of
Barack Obama as the president of the United States we
could move beyond centuries of racism and exploitation

---

6. Ibid., 53–54.

and have a post-racial America, and yet his election has brought forth some of the most vicious and unabashed racism that has been seen in decades; and at least in my estimation, things have gotten worse.

And if I could be really honest, I would tell you that I wrestle with despair. Despair that things will ever get better. Despair that our best hopes and dreams for freedom, liberation, equality, reconciliation, and access to the land and the resources for all will come to naught. The ability of a small minority of the human population that are globally wealthy to maneuver, manipulate, and always come out on top no matter what happens discourages me deeply.

Maybe I have been all my life too far on the side of the Angels of Love and Righteousness, believing that we will act lovingly and do righteous deeds, believing that we could do justice and love mercy. But I am right now in serious dialogue with the Angel of Truth. How can anyone ignore the truth: wickedness, deceit, war, violence, racism, global white privilege, trivializing of climate change, global warming, and issues of the de-valuing of the created order? Do you know that we are really stupid enough to drop nuclear warheads on ourselves? Someone asked Albert Einstein what weapons the third world war will be fought with. He said that he did not know, but he could tell you what the fourth world war would be fought with. He said, "Rocks."[7]

So, God, bring Truth back to heaven and close shop on this human experiment; heaven made a mistake by the creation of human beings. You remember that we have been at this point before. God, you got so frustrated with human beings that you sent a flood to virtually wipe everything out and start all over in Genesis 9. God you said in Genesis 9:11 that you would never flood the earth again,

---

7. Albert Einstein, in an interview with Alfred Werner, *Liberal Judaism* 16 (April–May 1949), Einstein Archive 30–1104, as sourced in *The New Quotable Einstein* by Alice Calaprice (Princeton, NJ: Princeton University Press, 2005), 173.

so we assume it will be by fire next time. Bring the fire, and let's be done with it. Just admit that heaven made a mistake. Burn, baby, burn! God, let the fire come. Heaven made a mistake. God, curse human beings and let us die. The human experiment did not work.

And then out of nowhere, out of the depths of my disappointment, hurt, anger, and despair, this text comes screaming to mind:

> ...and my soul is downcast within me. Yet this I call to mind and therefore I have hope: Because of the Lord's great love we are not consumed, for God's compassions never fail. They are new every morning; great is your faithfulness. (Lamentations 3:20-23 NIV)

It is owing to God and God alone that things are not worse. Because of the Lord's great love, we are not consumed. The steadfast love of the Lord never ceases. God's mercies never come to an end. They are new every morning. New every morning. Great is thy faithfulness. Everything would burn everything down except for one thing, the Lord's *hesed*—faithfulness.

I know that many are probably not familiar with the Hebrew term *hesed*, so let me explain. *Hesed* can be translated as lovingkindness, steadfast love, grace, mercy, and goodness. It means faithfulness to a relationship; to act in a loyal, loving way to a person. The word is used two hundred and forty times in the Old Testament, and comes up especially frequently in the Psalms. It is one of the most important terms in Hebrew theology and ethics. It means the strength of God, the steadfastness of God, and the love of God all taken together. God's love has to be full of strength and steadfastness to sustain the human enterprise.

Hesed means covenant love, involving mutual and reciprocal rights and obligations between the parties of a relationship, such as Yahweh and Israel. This covenant love is not based in obligation, but in generosity. In terms of God and Israel, the weaker party seeks the protection and blessing of the patron and protector, but may not deserve it. The stronger party remains committed to the covenant promise. *Hesed* goes beyond the rule of law; it is being in the relationship full of mercy, grace, steadfastness, and lovingkindness. God's lovingkindness is offered to the Israelites, who need redemption from sin, enemies, and trouble.

In Hebrew culture, someone does, shows, or keeps *hesed*. *Hesed* can operate in human relationship, but I don't have the time to focus on that. I want to talk about God: God does *hesed*. God does kindness. God does mercy. God does faithfulness. God does *hesed* in concrete acts of redemption in fulfilment of God's promise. God is *hesed*. God's *hesed* is so *hesed* that ultimately it is even beyond the covenant; it will not ultimately be abandoned, even when the human partner is unfaithful and must be disciplined. Because of the Lord's great love, we are not consumed. The steadfast love of the Lord never ceases. God's mercies never come to an end. They are new every morning. New every morning. Great is thy faithfulness. Everything would collapse except for one thing—the Lord's *hesed*—the Lord's lovingkindness—faithfulness.

This word *hesed* is used in Psalm 89:3 (NIV): "For I have said: The world is built on *hesed* (lovingkindness, mercy), in the very heavens you establish your faithfulness." The throne of God is established on *hesed*. Let me give you an image from Sandy Sasso and the rabbis. Have you ever been eating on a table, and one of the legs is wobbling? Maybe it was in a fine restaurant or maybe at home. You know that feeling? You have to put something like cardboard or a rock underneath the leg so that it will stop wobbling. Psalm 89:3: "For I have said: The world is built on *hesed*, in the very heavens you establish your faithfulness." The rabbi says that God's throne in heaven was wobbling and all of heaven was wobbling as well because one leg was too short until the Holy One, the Blessed One, propped it up. And with what did God prop up God's throne? *Hesed* (mercy). Hence it is said that the world is built on "mercy." Psalm 89:3: "For I have said: The world is built on mercy (*hesed*), in the very heavens you establish your faithfulness."

The world is like a throne with four legs; God's creation is likewise precarious, constantly tottering and wobbling between survival and extinction. Only *hesed*, mercy and divine grace, sustain existence. God props us up. If it were not for God's love, we would have already been consumed. The steadfast love of the Lord never ceases. God's mercies never come to an end. They are new every morning. New every morning. Great is thy faithfulness.

Let me get to our text in Lamentations 3:20-23. For eighteen straight months, Nebechudnezzar laid siege on Jerusalem. It got worse and worse, and the people suffered and suffered. Finally, Nebechudnezzar won the battle, and he completely demolished Jerusalem. The beloved Jerusalem went up in flames. Though it had been prophesied, the people were not ready for it. On top of the city burning, the Temple was destroyed; the Holy Temple of God was cast down. The people were taken away in slavery; there was unimaginable grief. The prophet personifies the grief of the people in his person starting in verse 1 of Lamentations 3:

> I am the man who has seen affliction by the rod of His wrath.
>
> God has led and brought me into darkness and not light.
>
> God has made my flesh and skin to waste away; He has broken my bones.
>
> God has hemmed me in, surrounding me with bitterness and anguish.

God has built a wall about me, and I cannot get out.

God has put heavy chains upon me. Even when I keep on crying and calling for help He shuts out my prayer.

God bent His bow and set me up as a target for His arrow. (13) He sent into my inward parts the shafts of His quiver.

God has filled me to the brim with bitterness, caused me to drink wormwood. (16) He has ground my teeth with gravel and covered me over with ashes.

Then verses 20-23:

...and my soul is downcast within me. Yet this I call to mind and therefore I have hope: Because of the LORD's (*hesed*) great love we are not consumed, for his compassions never fail. They are new every morning; great is your faithfulness.

Because of the Lord's kindness, we are not consumed. It is only because of God that things are not worse. It is the recognition of God's mercy that will not allow me to wreck my despair on others through violence and hate.

Because of the Lord's great kindness, we do not bust windows, set shops on fire, demonize police, hate, or physically or psychologically maim others. Because of the Lord's steadfast love, we go to police officers' funerals. Because of the Lord's *hesed*, we are nonviolent. We will address the issues. We will not back down, and we will not be intimidated. We will address these issues that dehumanize people and our planet, but because of the Lord's great love we are not violent, vindictive, or hateful. God's compassions never fail. They are new every morning. Great is thy faithfulness. We are the Lord's *hesed*

97

that holds the world up. When we go out to address the issues, we are the Lord's *hesed*. We stand for human dignity, decency, equality, love of creation, justice, mercy, and forgiveness. We declare, Heaven did not make a mistake! *Hesed* is greater than human mistakes. By our acts of mercy, compassion, and love, we slide mercy underneath the wobbling of the world.

Do you remember the story of Eric Garner, the young man who died in a chokehold by police in Brooklyn? You remember Garner saying, "I can't breathe." It ignited a movement with the slogan "I can't breathe" all over the country in protest. Do you remember that very weekend, two police officers were also assassinated in Brooklyn? Did you notice in the news coverage that the widow of Eric Garner, Esaw Garner, whose husband died in a chokehold by police, laid a wreath at the spot where those police officers were slain? The whole country was wobbling, but she propped the country up with mercy. Acts of kindness and forgiveness prop the country up. It is our calling to provide those acts of love and kindness as we march, protest, and stand up for justice.

Well, lest I keep you too long, *hesed* was not only in the Hebrew Bible, but *hesed* is in the New Testament as well. *Hesed* was a theological and ethical principle in the Hebrew Bible, and still is so in the New Testament, but most importantly, *hesed* became a person.

> He (Jesus) came—through forty and two generations;
> He came—Born on the backside of cheap motel;
> With wood shavings in his apron and carpenter tools
> in his belt he walked the dusty sands of Galilee—
> He came.
> He healed the sick
> Gave sight to the blind
> Made deaf folk hear
> Lame folk walk
> Brought dead folks back to life

But we soon discovered
The Angel of Truth was right
we would speak falsehood and contend even with Him
The Angel of Peace was right—
we are full of strife and we strove even with Him
So much so
That we crucified *hesed*
And the world began to tetter and totter
the world was wobbling
And we teetered between survival and extinction
Hesed had been removed
It was about the fall in
God was about to end it all
God turned up the furnace
God was about to end it all
But so deep and profound is the love of God
The faithfulness of God
The mercy of God
The *hesed* of God
that God raised *hesed* from the grave.
And *Hesed* reigns in glory
With all power in his hands
Hesed props up all mercy, justice, and love
Because of the Lord's Love we are not consumed
The steadfast love of the Lord never ceases
God's mercies never come to an end
Great is thy faithfulness
The resurrection props things back up
Heaven did not make a mistake....

THE FINAL WORD:

THE "FREEDOM FAITH" OF PRATHIA L. HALL (1940-2002)

I first met Prathia L. Hall in the mid 1980s at a gathering hosted by Vincent H. Harding in Colorado Springs, Colorado, to foster collegial networks of support and stimulate creative efforts of struggle for social change by linking religion and social transformation. Harding was a mentor; a kind, gentle spirit; a revolutionary warrior of peace; and a tireless advocate of the deep connections between the spiritual life and the work of social justice. He had been teacher, writer, professor, activist, and a partner and confidant of Martin Luther King Jr., and notably one of the writers of King's famous speech on April 3, 1967, "Beyond Vietnam," where King announced his controversial opposition to the Vietnam War. Harding summoned primarily a group of African Americans activists, ministers, leaders, teachers, and those who, in his words, "struggled for a new world."

When the group convened, one of the issues that surfaced unexpectedly, and yet quickly and viscerally, was the issue of the full participation of women in ministry. The women in the room affirmed and supported the right of every woman to minister as would any man. Several men in the room advocated some version of "women could be called to ministry but could not pastor," or some such limits on the ministry of women. Hall and several others went toe-to-toe with the men, and the conversation got emotional and deeply painful. Hall was succinct, clear, and obviously a veteran in standing up for herself and women. She was articulate, direct, profound, respectful, and would not give an inch. The discussion went forth and took much of the day, and eventually the entire gathering. I was in agreement that women have full and equal rights, but I sat there and said nothing. In the words of the Negro Spirituals, "never said a mumblin' word."

The next morning, I sat with Hall in the cafeteria for breakfast and we talked. I told her of my support for the cause of women. She told me that it was fine that I was in support, but if I were not going to say it in the room, then how did it help the cause? She was not angry or condescending. She challenged me and stated a truth that I needed to hear, and that we all need to hear every now and then if we are going to do moral ministry. It was easier for me to stay silent, and silence in this situation was a betrayal of what I believed. My silence was a violation of the first quality of moral imagination. I envisioned equality but did not demonstrate it in my physical presence. I did not show up. I was not fully present! I had it in my heart, but I would not embody it. I did not stand up. I was humbled and thanked her for the lesson and for the compassionate way that she called me into accountability. I struggled from there in the gathering, but I did speak. It was the beginning of finding my voice in such situations. From that conversation and gathering, Prathia L. Hall and I built a lasting relationship.

There is a strong movement to honor her memory and legacy in contemporary scholarship. I would like to make my contribution to honor her life and work and the powerful role of women in the struggle for freedom and equality. I want to give her the final and concluding word on moral imagination because she was such a visionary practicioner of the moral imagination.

Hall entitled the struggle for equality from her moral imagination as "freedom faith." I will present a brief biography, discuss the four qualities of the moral imagination in regard to freedom faith, and finally present the unpublished sermon "Freedom-Faith."

Brief Biography of Prathia L. Hall[1]

In the Fall of 1962, on a clear September day, members of the Student Nonviolent Coordinating Committee (SNCC), congregants of Mount Olive Baptist Church of Terrell County, Georgia, and others, even perhaps Martin Luther King Jr. and his associate James Bevel, stood before the smoldering ruins of the Mount Olive Church's building, one of three black church structures that had been burned to the ground within a two-week period. Bill Shipp, then-state-news editor for the *Atlanta Constitution* was moved by the prayer of a young civil rights activist named Prathia Laura Ann Hall. He recounts: "She prayed for God to help the Negroes raise from the ashes the walls of Mount Olive Church, Mount Mary's Church, and Shady Grove Baptist Church. She prayed for God to help those White men understand the Negro's problem." Then, says Shipp, "She turned her face toward the sky and cried out in an emotion-filled voice, 'We may not be free in our lifetime but, Oh, God, Lord in Heaven, one day, we're going to be free!' "[2]

Prathia L. Hall was born in 1940 in Philadelphia, Pennsylvania, as one of four children to Berkely and Ruby Hall. After college, Hall joined the Student Nonviolent Coordinating Committee (SNCC) to become one of the first women field leaders in Southwest Georgia. Hall was married and divorced and was the mother of a son and daughter. Her daughter died at age twenty-three due to a stroke.

Hall held master of divinity and doctoral degrees from Princeton Theological Seminary, Trenton, New Jersey. She specialized in womanist theology, ethics, and African American church history. She was an ordained American Baptist minister and also worked with the Progressive National Baptist Convention. She was a pioneering woman in ministry. In

---

1. For more information on Prathia L. Hall, see Martha Simmons and Frank A. Thomas, *Preaching with Sacred Fire: An Anthology of African American Sermons 1650–Present* (New York: W. W. Norton, 2010); Donna E. Allen, *Toward a Womanist Homiletic: Katie Canon, Alice Walker, and Emancipatory Proclamation* (New York: Peter Lang, 2014); Mittie K. Carey, "The Freedom Faith Speeches of Prathia L. Hall: Uncovering a Hybrid Rhetoric of Protest." PhD diss., University of Memphis, 2012; Courtney Pace Lyons, "'Freedom Faith': The Civil Rights Journey of Rev. Dr. Prathia Hall," PhD diss., Baylor University, 2011 (book forthcoming).

2. This story recounted by Carey, "The Freedom Faith Speeches," 9.

1978, she became the pastor of Rose of Sharon Baptist Church of Philadelphia, formerly pastored by her father. In 1982 she was the first woman received into membership of the Baptist Ministers' Conference of Philadelphia and Vicinity. She later was associate dean of spiritual and community life, director of the Harriet L. Miller Women's Center, and dean of African American ministries at United Theological Seminary in Dayton, Ohio, and also served as a visiting professor at ITC. She also served as an associate professor at Boston University School of Theology, holding the Martin Luther King Jr. Chair in Social Ethics.

When *Ebony* magazine presented its only list of the Outstanding African American Women Preachers in America in 1997, Prathia Hall was listed first. Hall was a revivalist, which as late as 2002 was still a rare achievement for women preachers of any race.

The height of compliment was paid to Hall's preaching when Martin Luther King Jr. said "Prathia Hall is one platform speaker, I would not like to follow."[3] Scholars acknowledge that King incorporated the phrase, "I have a dream" in his speeches after hearing it from the dynamic speaking of Prathia L. Hall.[4]

"Freedom Faith" and Four Qualities of Moral Imagination

It is clear that what I describe as the four qualities of moral imagination is very similar to what Prathia L. Hall termed "freedom faith." I would like to briefly establish her definition of freedom faith, and then draw necessary parallels to the four qualities of the moral imagination.

According to Mittie K. Carey, Hall first coined the phrase, freedom faith, in 1997, but described it as early as 1965 as she witnessed the

3. "Prathia Hall," *This Far by Faith: African American Spiritual Journeys*, PBS, accessed March 31, 2017, http://www.pbs.org/thisfarbyfaith/people/prathia_hall.html.

4. The Center for African American Religious Research and Education, "Inaugural Events Dedicated to the Late BU Theology Prof. Prathia Hall," news release, October 2, 2003, http://www.bu.edu/news/2003/09/26/boston-university-school-of-theology-launches-center-for-african-american-religious-research-and-education/.

courage and resilience of local black residents and their supporters in the Deep South in their fight against racial oppression. Hall believed that these freedom fighters's ability to blend their longing for social, political, and economic freedom with their Christian faith was the spiritual force that kept them in the struggle. Hall says:

> The local people...had the wisdom of the ages, which they so generously shared with us. They had lived in this system of brutal racial injustice all of their lives, and for their generations past. And somehow, they found a way to survive. Not only to remain physically alive, but to remain psychically, and spiritually alive.... [How] had they done that? They had done that because each generation had passed on to the next generation this thing that I call freedom faith. This sense that I'm not a nigger...I'm not a gal, I'm not boy. I am God's child....And so they managed to live amid those dangers, and to experience the brutality, and all the rest of it, and still remain whole. Because their wholeness was something which transcended the realities which they were living in their daily lives. And so from somewhere beyond them and somewhere deeply within them came this courage...to get up in a meeting, and say, "I'm afraid. It may cost my job, it may cost my life, but I want to be free, and I want my children to be free. So I'm going down to the courthouse, and I'm going to sign my name. And I'm going to trust God to take me there, and I'm going to trust God to bring me back." That's courage. That's faith. That's freedom faith.[5]

Hall created the term freedom faith in her doctoral dissertation (1998) and consistently speaks of freedom and faith as a single utterance, and not two distinct words. By doing so, she melds two belief systems, one sociopolitical and one religious. She means that the desire for freedom alone was not sufficient to keep disenfranchised blacks in the struggle, nor was their faith standing alone sufficient enough. As Carey says, it was the "hybridization" of the two belief systems that motivated freedom fighters to stay in the struggle, despite overwhelming odds and risks.[6]

Not only was freedom faith a catalyst for activism on behalf of the struggle for black freedom, but also for women, and specifically, black women. The large involvement of black women in civil rights activism

---

5. Carey, 9.

6. Ibid.

symbolized in the voice, person, and actions of women such as Gwendolyn Zorah Simmons, Ella Baker, Diane Nash, Ruby Neil Sales, Septima Clarke, and so many others who spoke to freedom from white oppression and deliverance from patriarchy, and especially the patriarchy of the black church. There has developed in these latter years, much more accurate and insightful scholarship of the role of black women in freedom struggles, not only in the civil rights movement, but in freedom struggles throughout the long sojourn of black people in America.

Hall's definition of freedom faith includes the four qualities of the moral imagination. First, it is obvious by virtue of marches, protests, boycotts, going to jail, and so on, that she envisioned equality and represented it by her physical presence. Secondly, she saw empathy, sacrifice, and death as a catalyst or bridge to create opportunities to overcome the past and make new decisions for peace and justice. The sacrifices made by Hall and so many for the freedom struggle created and engendered an empathy within themselves and many people of goodwill to eradicate injustice. Thirdly, Hall found wisdom in ancient texts such as the Bible, and sources of ancient wisdom, and as Hall says several paragraphs ago, "they passed the wisdom of the ages down from generation to generation." Finally, Hall spoke, as you will see in this closing sermon, the language of poetry and art that lifts and elevates and creates wonder, mystery, and hope in the hearts of people. She simply was a phenomenal preacher.

In the presentation of this sermon, "Freedom-Faith," you will capture the sense of the four qualities of the moral imagination that we have been discussing in these many pages. It is my hope that they inspire and encourage you to preach a dangerous sermon from the moral imagination in your context. Remember!—

Moral imagination is the ability of the preacher, intuitive or otherwise, in the midst of the chaotic experiences of human life and existence, to grasp and share God's abiding wisdom and ethical truth in order to benefit the individual and common humanity.

"FREEDOM-FAITH"

PRATHIA L. HALL

DELIVERED MARCH 23, 2000

BROWN CHAPEL AME CHURCH

SELMA, ALABAMA

Good Morning. How very good it is to say good morning. In the name of the one who won the victory at Calvary [*sic*]. I'm so very happy to again be in this wonderful
place, to again stand on this holy ground. And Pastor Har-
ris, I do genuinely thank you for your gracious hospitality
and for the graciousness of this preaching place. Thanks
be to God. I ask you to hear the word of the Lord as given
to us in the letter of Paul to the Galatian Christians. Gala-
tians Chapter 5, verses 1, 13, and 14:

> For freedom that Christ has set us free. Stand firm,
> then and do not submit again, to a yoke of slav-
> ery. For you were called to freedom, brothers and
> sisters; only do not use your freedom as a means
> for self-indulgence, but through love, become
> slaves one to another. For the whole lot is summed
> up in a single commandment. "You shall love your
> neighbor as yourself."

This, beloved, is the word of God for the people of God.
Thanks be to God.

I have come to this place, made holy by the blood of
freedom's martyrs, to talk about Freedom Faith. The last
time I stood in Brown Chapel African Methodist Episcopal

107

Church, the stench of tear gas was in the air. Blood covered the heads and the faces of those who had been beaten bloody by the clubs of Jim Clark's posse and the so-called Alabama state safety patrol. People were sobbing, screaming in pain and in shock. That day in March 1965 has gone down in history as Bloody Sunday. And now pilgrims come from across the world to Selma, to Brown Chapel, to remember.

Now I ask you on this bright, sunny Sunday in March in the year 2000, why did so many put their lives at risk? They knew when they set out for the Edmond Pettus Bridge that segregation storm troopers were waiting for them. Yet, they set their faces toward Montgomery in much the same way that Jesus set his face toward Jerusalem. A mock trial, humiliation, scourging, which was infinitely more brutal than a beating. Suffering, agony, anguish, Calvary and death awaited him. And yet, He turned neither to the left nor to the right. But the scripture says, "Set His face like a flint toward Jerusalem." Why did He do it? Paul says in this morning's text that He did it for freedom.

For Freedom Christ has set me free. And indeed, the marches on the Selma Bridge did the same thing. Through the blood, through the pain, though the tears, John Louis, Bob Manse, Jose Williams, and so many more utter their rebellious testimony, "I woke up this morning with my mind stayed on freedom. I'm walking and talking with my mind stayed on freedom. Ain't no harm, to keep your mind stayed on freedom. Hallelu, Hallelu, Hallelu, Hallelu." They sang as did our slave foreparents, "Oh, freedom, oh, freedom over me. And before I'll be a slave, I'll be buried in my grave, and go home to my Lord and be free."

Those freedom marchers of 1965, moved out in the spirit of Jesus, and in the spirit and faith of their ancestors. They moved out in faith, and with a faith that had been formed over hundreds of years in the crucible of suffering and struggle. It was a Freedom Faith. A faith in freedom. A faith for freedom. Grounded in the absolute, positive, without a doubt conviction that God intended them to be free. That God had brought them to that time, and that place, and that hour in history to boldly confront the bedrock forces of segregation and racial injustice. The forces of death. And, they were convinced that God was right now, standing with them. And therefore they would not go down in defeat. God in heaven knows they did not.

That was the faith which burned deeply in the souls of our African American ancestors. That faith in freedom. A central principle in African American religious belief enabled them to survive the cruelty and brutality of the Middle Passage, slavery, lynching, terror, segregation, discrimination, Jim Crow, Jane Crow, denial and duplicity. And yet, remain whole persons. Who though bloody and cast down, were not destroyed. It's amazing isn't it? It's amazing. Yes, it is amazing. The Freedom Faith of our ancestors still burned within us thirty-five years ago, and strengthened us to do battle with the extraordinarily powerful forces of racial and economic injustice until, before our very eyes, walls came tumbling. It is amazing.

But the scripture does not allow us to rest upon the Freedom Faith of our foremothers and forefathers. It has a compelling word to us right now. Indeed it has a word for us as we march into [*sic*] the twenty-first century. Paul follows his declaration of freedom in Christ with the admonition, "Stand firm, therefore, in the freedom where with Christ has set you free and do not submit again to a yoke of slavery." Now it's one thing to salute the awesome courage, vision, and determination of our foremother and forefather. But, my sisters and my brothers, what is this business about standing firm in the present tense? Stand firm in your freedom, says the text, and do not submit to another yoke of bondage. Could this text possibly make reference to our handling of the legacy of freedom struggles today? Stand firm? Why some of us are slipping and sliding so badly we do not even wish to remember freedom struggle. There is regularly before us some new wave, post-modern authority telling us to move forward without looking back. "Don't dwell on the past," they offer. They say, "Thinking about the past will make you bitter. Go forward. Don't keep bringing up that old pain." I can only admonish these sad souls, that really knowing our past does not make us bitter, it makes us better. When we know what we've come from, when we then regain the necessary coping skills to go through what we must go through and our children are desperately in need of those skills.

Some of us have so relaxed our hold on freedom's plow that we do not even bother to register to vote. "All those politicians are all the same," they say. "My vote will not make a difference." Yes, you're absolutely right, your vote will not make a difference unless you use it. Right now, the black population of Washington, DC, is fighting for voting rights. Some of us have permitted our eyes to give up the fight for economic freedom before we have even begun the struggle. We have robbed our children of their stories, because we have refused to pass unto them, what was passed on to us. Do you really believe, sisters and brothers, that our babies would be killing each other, and themselves, if they really knew who they were? If they really knew how precious the price with which they have been bought? If they really knew that they are too rare, too lovely, our only hope of a future, to expend their lives in drugs and violence? We must tell them, we must tell them how it is that we have come this far by faith. We must tell them. We must tell them, that for freedom, Christ hath made you free. That for freedom, the warriors of Selma, Birmingham, Alabama, of Albany, Jacksonville, and Macomb, and Danville, have set you free. Stand firm, therefore, and do not submit to another yoke of slavery. Sisters and Brothers, the battle is not over.

The challenges to us remain before us. We are challenged regarding our commitment. We are called to action right now. We are not to use these blessings with which—which have been purchased with the blood of the martyrs, to simply indulge our appetite for more things. We are called to use the wonderful resources which we now enjoy more that our visionary parents could even dream about. To continue freedom's struggle. To rescue our children. To set them on the road to full empowerment as human beings who have been set free for freedom. We have been free, that we might set free.

And there is much work to be done. Stand firm, therefore, and do not submit to another yoke of slavery. Whether it is drugs or guns, or credit cards, cancer, or dehumanizing relationship, or poor self-esteem, or apathy, complacency, or ignorance. Do not submit. Stand first in the Freedom Faith of our mothers and fathers. In the Freedom Faith of our elders. In the freedom which we have in Christ. And let us know as Ella Baker taught us, "We who believe in freedom cannot rest. We who believe in freedom cannot rest! We who believe in freedom cannot rest" until it comes.